SIX-MINUTE SCIENCE
EXPERIMENTS

FAITH HICKMAN BRYNIE

Illustrations by Kim Whittingham

Sterling Publishing Co., Inc.
New York

Dedication

To Lloyd, who taught me how to make silly sand and has been sharing the fun ever since.

Library of Congress Cataloging-in-Publication Data

Brynie, Faith Hickman, 1946–
    Six-minute science experiments / Faith Hickman Brynie ;
illustrated by Kim Whittingham.
            p.   cm.
        Includes index.
        Summary: Provides instructions for more than twenty simple science
experiments such as planting seeds upside down, dyeing a white shirt
gold, and discovering how a pendulum works.
        ISBN 0-8069-0624-3
        1. Science—Experiments—Juvenile literature. [1. Science
—Experiments. 2. Experiments.] I. Whittingham, Kim, ill.
II. Title.
Q164.B9   1996
507.8—dc20   95-24478
                                                                                    CIP
                                                                                    AC

1   3   5   7   9   10   8   6   4   2
Published by Sterling Publishing Company, Inc.
387 Park Avenue South, New York, N.Y. 10016
© 1996 by Faith Hickman Brynie
Distributed in Canada by Sterling Publishing
℅ Canadian Manda Group, One Atlantic Avenue, Suite 105
Toronto, Ontario, Canada M6K 3E7
Distributed in Great Britain and Europe by Cassell PLC
Wellington House, 125 Strand, London WC2R 0BB, England
Distributed in Australia by Capricorn Link (Australia) Pty Ltd.
P.O. Box 6651, Baulkham Hills, Business Centre, NSW 2153, Australia
Printed in Hong Kong
All rights reserved

Sterling ISBN 0-8069-0624-3

Table of Contents

Before You Begin

Welcome to six-minute science. Between these covers you'll find science experiments you can set up and finish in a flash, but don't be surprised if you're still working on them hours later. Why? Because these experiments will get you started, and after a while your own questions and ideas may lead you deeper into science topics that interest you.

And there's a lot of science here to explore. You will find out about the chemistry of acids and bases and learn how some animals escape hungry predators. You will make gases fill balloons, frogs balance on high wires, and bubbles go from round to square. You will separate green into yellow and blue, make a "goop" that flows like water yet crumbles in your fist, track smells that only your nose knows, build a race car, plant seeds upside down, dye a white shirt gold, and build a musical instrument. You'll find out how levers, pendulums, electrical circuits, and human hearts work. You'll even learn how snakes and rabbits survive winter's cold.

All these experiments and more await you in these pages. You'll find plenty to do here, and we hope you'll have fun experimenting. That's what six-minute science is all about!

BERRY, BERRY, NOT SO CONTRARY

Ah, Sunday breakfast! A great chance to relax. Blueberry muffins, grape juice, and the Sunday comics.

Hey, wait a minute! Before you get too comfortable, those blueberries and that grape juice are just what you need to do some six-minute science! You'd better race to the kitchen before somebody throws out the juice from the blueberry can!

YOU NEED

- juice from one can of blueberries or about ½ cup (120 ml) purple grape juice
- set of measuring spoons
- 1 dessert spoon
- measuring cup
- 3 small transparent glasses
- 1–2 teaspoons baking soda
- 1–2 tablespoons white vinegar
- water
- 1 piece of paper
- pencil

WHAT TO DO

1. You can use either blueberry juice or grape juice. You don't need both. If you use canned blueberries, drain the juice from the can into a cup or glass.

2. Pour ¼ cup (60 ml) of blueberry juice or grape juice into a measuring cup.

3. Add water up to the one cup mark. Stir.

4. Put two tablespoons of this juice and water mixture into each of three small, clear glasses.

5. On a piece of paper, write CONTROL. On another, write ACID. On a third, write BASE. (These words won't mean much to you yet, but they will soon.) Slip the pieces of paper under the glasses.

6. Using a measuring spoon, add ⅛ teaspoon of white vinegar to the glass marked ACID. Watch the color. Does it change? If it does not, add a little more vinegar.

7. Add ⅛ teaspoon of baking soda to the glass marked BASE. Does the color change? If not, add a tiny bit more. See any difference?

8. Now compare the colors in the ACID and BASE glasses to the CONTROL glass. Do acids like vinegar change the color of the juice? How about a base like baking soda?

9. Blueberry juice and grape juice are good IN-DICATORS. An indicator is a chemical that changes color when it's mixed with other chemicals. Your juicy indicator tells you whether chemicals are acids or bases. Acids and bases do interesting things. Let's do some experiments to see what they are.

Let's Experiment!

YOU NEED

⟶ assortment of house-hold cleaners (win-dow cleaner, floor cleaner, dishwashing liquid, etc.)

⟶ 1 lemon

⟶ 1 can of clear soft drink (such as 7-Up)

WHAT TO DO

1. Use your blueberry or grape juice indicator to test unknown liquids. The color change will tell you whether the liquid is an acid or a base. Try testing lemon juice, clear soft drinks, dishwashing pow-ders or liquids, or liquid cleaners. *Important: Before you test any cleaners, check with an adult. Some house-*

hold chemicals can burn your skin or stain your clothes.

2. Keep the three glasses you made before to help you remember colors. Make up some new glasses, putting two tablespoons of indicator in each one.

3. Make paper labels with the names of the chemicals you want to test. Put the labels under the glasses.

4. Start by adding a tiny amount of what you want to test to the indicator. If nothing happens, add a little more. Can you tell which are acids and which are bases from the color?

Handy Hints

☞ It's a good idea to test chemicals that are clear or light in color. Dark liquids like colas make the color change hard to see.

☞ There is nothing but indicator in the glass marked CONTROL, but it is the most important glass of all. Can you see why?

WANT TO DO MORE?

⇒ Do you ever have red cabbage for dinner? Next time, save some of the water it was cooked in. Is red cabbage water an indicator? How can you find out? What other indicators can you find?

⇒ What happens when acids and bases mix? Put two tablespoons of vinegar in a glass. Set the glass in the sink or a big bowl. (You'll see why!) Now add a teaspoon of baking soda. What happens? Try it again, but put indicator in first. Is there a color change?

⇒ Use vinegar and baking soda to make a volcano. *Work in the sink or outside— this can get messy.* Make a volcano cone from modeling clay or cardboard. Think of a way to mix vinegar and baking soda inside so that your volcano "erupts."

Why-Oh-Why?

What makes one liquid an acid and another a base?

Why do indicators change color?

What happens when acids and bases combine?

Turn to page 70 to find out.

WHEN IS OH-TWO NOT OH-TOO?

Have you ever flown in a balloon? What makes it rise? It's hot air that does it. There's a burner at the base of the balloon that heats the air inside. As the air gets warmer, the balloon rises.

Hot air isn't the only way to blow up a balloon. Have you ever bought a balloon filled with helium? Hang on, or it will get away!

Have you ever thought about the hot air and the helium inside balloons? You can't see anything in there, but you know something must be there. How do you know? Because the balloon gets bigger as it fills up with air or helium. Helium is a GAS. Air is a mixture of several GASES.

If you have six minutes, you can make two other gases. You won't be able to see them, but you'll know they're there!

YOU NEED

- 2 tall, narrow-necked bottles
- 1 small plastic funnel
- 2 balloons
- 1 teaspoon baking soda
- 1 teaspoon dry yeast
- ⅛ cup (30 ml) vinegar
- ⅛ cup (30 ml) hydrogen peroxide
- 2 toothpicks
- set of measuring spoons
- measuring cup
- masking tape
- pen
- sink or pan to work in

WHAT TO DO

Caution: Hydrogen peroxide is a poison. Do not get it in your eyes or mouth. Do not use peroxide without permission from an adult.

1. Clean out the bottles. Make sure you can fit the balloons over the tops of your bottles.

2. Tear off two pieces of masking tape. On the first, write "Baking soda and vinegar." On the second, write "Yeast and peroxide." Tape the labels onto the bottles.

3. Put the funnel over the mouth of the first bottle, the one marked "Baking soda and vinegar." Put the baking soda into the funnel. Work it down into the bottle by "stirring" with a toothpick.

4. Put the bottle in a pan or sink.

5. This part can get messy. Get ready to move quickly. Pour the vinegar through the funnel into the bottle. As soon as the vinegar is in the bottle, remove the funnel and slide the balloon onto the bottle, as shown.

6. Hold the balloon in place so it doesn't slip off the bottle or leak. Watch what happens to the balloon. If you were slow in getting the balloon on, you

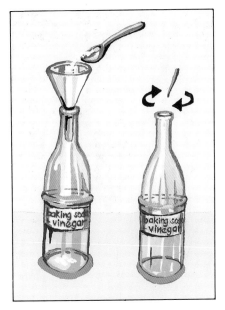

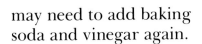

may need to add baking soda and vinegar again.

7. Wash and dry your measuring cup, measuring spoons, and funnel for the next part of the experiment.

8. Add the yeast into the bottle labelled "Yeast and peroxide."

9. Put the bottle in the sink or in a pan.

10. Add the hydrogen peroxide to the yeast through the funnel.

11. Quickly, remove the funnel. Slip the balloon over the top of the bottle. If things move slowly, try swirling the bottle gently.

12. Watch what happens.

13. You've made a gas inside each bottle. How can you tell?

9

Let's Experiment!

YOU NEED

- 1 narrow-necked bottle
- 1 balloon
- water

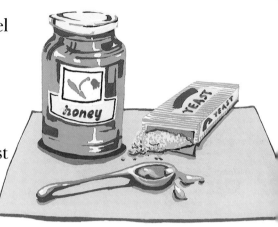

- 1 small plastic funnel
- set of measuring spoons
- measuring cup
- 1 teaspoon honey
- ½ teaspoon dry yeast
- masking tape
- pen

WHAT TO DO

1. Clean out one of your bottles. Make a new label that says "Yeast and honey."

2. Pour about ¼ cup (60 ml) of the water into a measuring cup. Add the honey to the cup. You can use a teaspoon of regular sugar if you don't have any honey. Stir the honey or sugar into the water until it is well mixed.

3. Pour the honey-water or sugar-water into the bottle.

4. Add the yeast through the funnel.

5. Fit a balloon over the top of the bottle. Let it sit several hours in a warm place. What happens?

Handy Hints

☞ You may need to shop around for balloons that have big enough holes to fit over the tops of the bottles you are using.

☞ The more ingredients you use, the more gas you will make. You can make your balloons blow up very large.

WANT TO DO MORE?

➡ Can these balloons take you up, up, and away? Try it and see. Tie off the balloons and remove them from the bottles. Set them sailing through the air. What happens?

Why-Oh-Why?

Where did your gases come from and what are they called?

Turn to page 70 to find out.

TIGHTROPE WALKER

The band stops playing. A hush falls over the crowd. High above in the big top, the tightrope walker bows. She carries a long, curved stick with knobs on the ends. Slowly, she steps onto the rope. One foot in front of the other, she moves across vast, open space with only the thin rope to hold her. She tips to the left. The audience gasps as she regains her balance. She tips dangerously to the right. The long pole seems to pull her down towards the safety net below.

Balancing on a tightrope is hard enough, but to carry that big, long pole must make it even harder. Right?

Maybe not. Maybe that tightrope walker knows her science. Take six minutes to discover her secret.

YOU NEED

➡ scissors
➡ 1 file folder
➡ 10 paper clips
➡ 3 sheets of white paper
➡ 1 sheet of carbon paper
➡ transparent tape
➡ pencil

WHAT TO DO

1. Trace the diamond and the frog from the next page onto white paper.

2. Use carbon paper to trace the shapes onto a file folder.

3. Use scissors to cut the shapes out of the file folder.

4. Try to balance the diamond by its point on your finger or on the table.

5. Slide one or two paper clips onto the end of each frog leg.

6. Balance your frog by its point on your finger or on the edge of the table. Move the paper clips until you are happy with the balance. The frog balances but the diamond doesn't. Why? Try some experiments to find out.

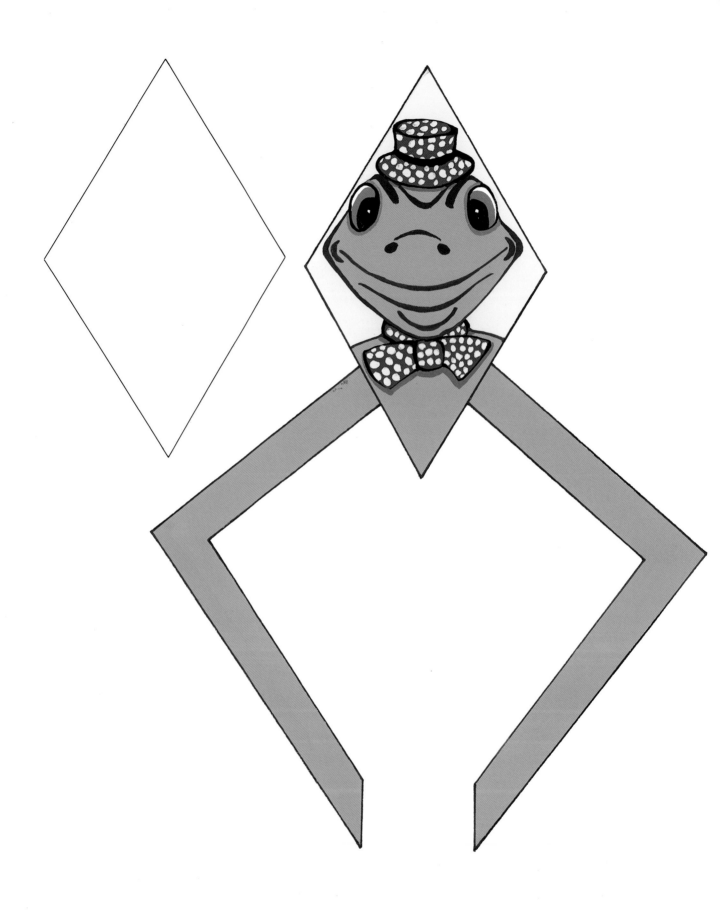

Let's Experiment!

WHAT TO DO

1. Trace this frog shape onto a file folder. Try balancing it. Is it easier or harder to balance than the first frog you made?

2. Try cutting some shapes of your own and taping them to the diamond. What must you do to make it balance? What shapes make it easier to balance?

WANT TO DO MORE?

➥ Make a potato or a lemon balance on a pencil point. Two forks should do it, but where will you put them?

➥ Trace the elephant shape from page 11. Make a pole to make it balance on your finger.

Handy Hints

☞ If your frog balances but leans to one side, try turning the paper clips in opposite directions.

☞ Sometimes, the frog balances better if you add more paper clips. Try stringing them together and letting them hang from the frog's legs.

☞ You need to use the same size and number of paper clips on both sides. Why?

Why-Oh-Why?

Why does your frog balance while your diamond does not?

Why is that tightrope walker better off with her pole than without it?

Teeter on over to page 71 to find out.

DOUGH, DOUGH, MOLD, AND GO

Oh, *what to do, what to do! It's a rainy day. There's nothing on TV. There's nothing interesting to play with. No money to go anywhere or buy any new toys.*

Don't be blue. You don't need money. All you need is some six-minute science to make a modeling dough that's just as good as the expensive store-bought kind. Ask permission to use a few things in the kitchen. Then you're off and running!

YOU NEED

- 1¼ cups (150 g) all-purpose flour
- ¾ cup (240 g) of salt
- 2 teaspoons cream of tartar
- ½ cup (120 ml) water
- vegetable oil
- measuring cup
- set of measuring spoons
- bowl
- 1 large spoon

WHAT TO DO

1. Stir the flour, the salt, and the cream of tartar in a bowl until they are well mixed.

2. Add the water and 4 teaspoons of the vegetable oil to the mixture. Stir well. When the dough starts to get stiff, mix it with your hands.

3. If your modeling dough is too stiff, add a few drops of vegetable oil. If it is too soft, add a little more flour.

4. Work your dough until it holds the shapes you give it. Smell it. What makes the nice smell? Feel it. Why are these things so different when they are mixed together than when they were apart?

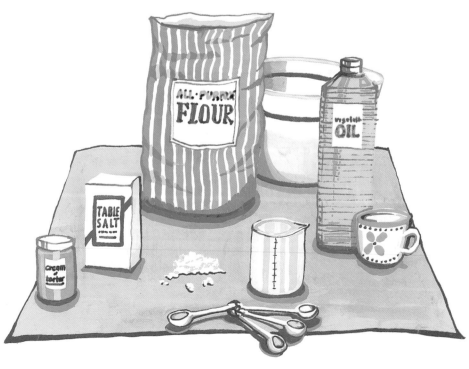

5. You can do lots of things with your dough. Here are just a few ideas to try:

➠ Make a flat, pancake shape from your dough. Press your hand into it. Press hard enough to make a deep print of all your fingers. Try the same thing with your feet and toes. Make hand and toe pancakes every few months and you'll have a record of how you grow.

➠ Make geometric shapes from your dough—flat squares, circles, rectangles, triangles, pentagons, and hexagons. Now make solid shapes—cubes, spheres, cylinders, and pyramids (try three-sided and four-sided bases).

Let's Experiment!

YOU NEED

➠ diet scale

WHAT TO DO

Want to preserve your creations for years to come? Do an experiment to compare drying methods.

1. Make three shapes all exactly alike. (To be accurate, use a diet scale to weigh three equal amounts of dough.)

2. Bake one shape in a microwave. Try full power for one minute for flat shapes or two minutes for solids.

3. Bake a second shape in the oven at 400°F (200°C) for 20 minutes.

4. Let a third shape dry in the air for three or four days.

How do the results compare? Is one drying method better than another?

Handy Hints

☞ Your modeling dough will stay fresh for weeks if you seal it in a plastic container. You don't need to refrigerate it, but be sure you put the lid on!

☞ After your dough shapes are hard, color them with felt-tipped markers or crayons. You can give them a shiny finish with clear fingernail polish.

WANT TO DO MORE?

➡ Make a wall hanging or mobile. Pick a science theme—maybe animal shapes or stars or flowers. Form the shapes you want from modeling dough, bake, and color them. Be sure to make a hole for the string to go through. Tie your shapes together and hang them from a coat hanger or on the wall. Shapes hung outdoors make a clanky wind chime.

Why-Oh-Why?

How and why do water, flour, and oil change when mixed together?

Why does heat harden mixtures?

Look for some answers on page 71.

BUBBLING OVER

Bubbles in the dishpan. Bubbles in the bath. Bubbles in ocean waves and stagnant ponds. Where else have you seen bubbles? Are bubbles all alike? Have you ever seen a square bubble? Can you make red bubbles? Try some six-minute science and find out.

YOU NEED

- measuring cup
- 3 cups of water
- 1 spoon
- ½ cup (120 ml) dishwashing liquid
- 8 pipe cleaners
- 10 straws
- 12 inches (30 cm) of string
- set of food colors
- 1 tall, plastic container (the kind used for ice cream or frozen yogurt) or a bucket

WHAT TO DO

1. In a tall, plastic container, mix the dishwashing liquid with the water.

2. Use a pipe cleaner to make a heart-shaped bubble blower.

3. Dip the blower in the soap. Get a thin film of soap inside the heart. Blow gently. Do you get a heart-shaped bubble?

4. Try making a long, thin bubble. Dip the end of a soda straw in your bubble soap and blow gently through the straw. What happens? Can you think of a reason why?

5. Try making pipe-cleaner bubble blowers in other shapes. What hap-

pens when you blow?

6. Make square and triangular bubble blowers by running string through short segments of straws. (Cut the straws short so your frame can fit in your soap container.)

7. Swing your frames

through the air or blow through them. What shape bubbles do you get?

8. Add several drops of food coloring to your bubble soap. What happens to the color of your bubbles?

Are you ready to make square bubbles?

Let's Experiment!

YOU NEED

⟹ cookie sheet or paper plate

⟹ 20–30 toothpicks

⟹ small ball of modeling clay

⟹ modeling dough from "Dough, Dough, Mold and Go"

WHAT TO DO

1. Working on a cookie sheet or paper plate, build a cube with toothpicks. A cube has six, square sides. Use little balls of modeling clay to hold the corners together.

2. Once you have the shape right, replace the modeling clay with the dough you made for "Dough, Dough, Mold, and Go." Work on the cookie sheet that you're going to use in the oven (or the paper plate you'll use in the microwave) so that you won't have to lift your cube onto it later.

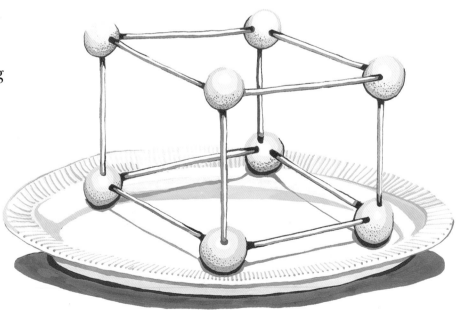

3. Microwave (on the paper plate) or bake (on the cookie sheet) your cube until the dough is hard. Microwaving takes a minute or two. You'll need about ten minutes in the regular oven at 400°F (200°C). This will give you a cube that won't fall apart.

4. After the cube has baked and cooled, dip it into your bubble mixture.

Make sure it goes completely below the surface of the bubble soap. Keep your fingers on the edges. Carefully, lift the cube out. What bubbles do you see inside?

5. Next, build a pyramid out of toothpicks with a three-sided base. Then build one with a four-sided base. Dip them in soap. What bubble shapes do you get?

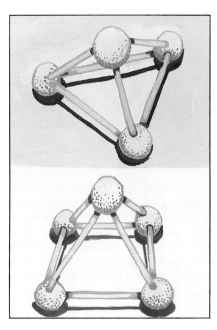

WANT TO DO MORE?

➡ Get permission to work on a table top that won't be hurt by soap. Put a spoonful of bubble soap on the table. Put a straw in the soap and blow through gently until you've made a dome-shaped bubble on the table top. Make it as big as you can. Now, blow other bubbles inside the dome. Keep practicing. You can do it!

➡ Build toothpick and modeling-dough structures with as many twists, turns, and odd angles as you can. Dip them in bubble soap to see what beautiful shapes you can make.

Handy Hints

☞ Bubbles burst when they dry out. They also burst when they come in contact with dry clothes, table tops, and dry fingers. Keep your hands wet with bubble soap when you dip.

☞ If your fingers get in the way of dipping, tie a piece of string around the cube and pyramids. Use it to lower the shapes into the soap.

☞ Bubbles are stronger and last longer if you add a spoonful of glycerin to the bubble soap. You can get it at the drugstore.

Why-Oh-Why?

What makes bubbles round?

Do the same forces make square bubbles?

If you're bubbling over with questions, turn to page 72.

WHEN GREEN'S NOT GREEN

What happens when you mix paints? Try mixing yellow and red. What do you get? What happens when you mix yellow and blue? Once colors are mixed, can you separate them again? In six minutes, you can find out.

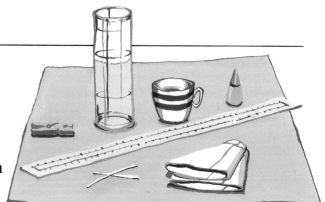

YOU NEED

⟹ small bottle of green food color

⟹ 2 coffee filters

⟹ ruler

⟹ 1 tall glass

⟹ 1 small cup

⟹ 1 toothpick

⟹ 1 clothespin

⟹ water

WHAT TO DO

1. Put a drop of green food coloring in a little cup.

2. Cut a long, narrow strip across the middle of the coffee filter. Make the strip a little over an inch (3 cm) wide.

3. Use a toothpick to "paint" a little dot of food coloring on the paper, a little over an inch (3 cm) from the bottom of the strip.

4. Let the dot dry.

5. Put a small amount of water in the bottom of a

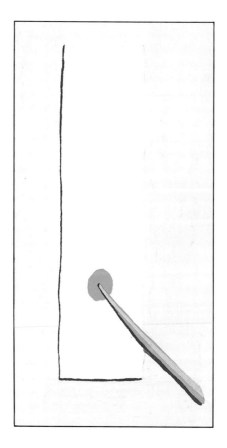

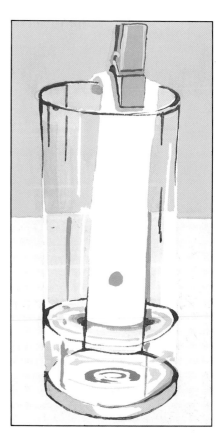

glass. The water should rise less than an inch (2 cm) in the bottom of the glass.

6. Hang the paper strip over the side of the glass, so that the bottom of the paper just touches the water. Be careful not to get the green dot in the water.

7. Fold the towel over the edge of the glass. Clip it in place with a clothespin.

8. Watch what happens as the water climbs the paper strip. What happens to the green color?

Let's Experiment!

YOU NEED

➡ 1 brown paper towel

WHAT TO DO

1. Get a piece of brown paper towel from a school or public restroom.

2. Cut a strip of the towel. Paint a dot of green food coloring on it. Hang it over the edge of a glass with a little water, as before.

3. After the water has risen and the colors have separated, lay the strip beside the white, filter paper you made before. The strips are different. Can you see how?

Handy Hints

☞ Try McCormick® food coloring. Some other brands don't work.

☞ You can use some kinds of paper towel instead of a coffee filter, but stay away from the very soft, fluffy kind. Colors don't separate well on them.

☞ Be careful with food coloring. It stains clothes and furniture.

Why-Oh-Why?

Why do some colors travel farther up the paper than others?

You'll find the answer to that question and more on page 72.

WANT TO DO MORE?

➡ Try separating the colors in felt-tip pens and markers. Permanent markers seem to work better than the washable kind, but one washable brown separated into a beautiful purple and yellow. Black can offer some interesting surprises, too.

➡ Try witch hazel instead of water in the glass. (*Do not get witch hazel in your mouth. It is a poison.*) Sometimes, it causes colors to separate differently than water does.

CHOP-AND-GLOP

Hard as a rock. Flowing like a stream. It's easy to tell solids from liquids. Or is it?

Have you ever thought about what makes a solid solid? Why is it that a liquid is a liquid?

One thing you know for sure about solids—they don't change their shape, at least not easily.

Liquids are different. They don't have a shape of their own. They take the shape of whatever holds them.

What else makes solids and liquids different? Are some things both solid and liquid? To find out, make some chop-and-glop.

YOU NEED

⟹ cornstarch
⟹ water (cold)
⟹ 1 spoon
⟹ bowl
⟹ set of measuring spoons
⟹ 1 plastic bag
⟹ 2 paper cups
⟹ 1 dinner knife
⟹ set of food colors

WHAT TO DO

Caution: This experiment can get messy. Work in the kitchen sink or somewhere outside where cleanup is not a problem.

1. Measure one cup (140 gr) cornstarch into a bowl.

2. Pour ½ cup (120 ml) water into the bowl.

3. Mix with a spoon until very smooth.

4. Test your chop-and-glop by running a knife through it. The knife should leave a cut mark that disappears in a few seconds. If the cut mark stays, add a teaspoon more water. If no cut mark forms, add a teaspoon more cornstarch. Keep adding cornstarch or water until your chop-and-

glop passes the knife test. You are now ready to find out if chop-and-glop is a solid, a liquid, or something else.

5. Try many different tests on your chop-and-glop. You'll have lots of ideas of your own. Here are just a few to get you started:

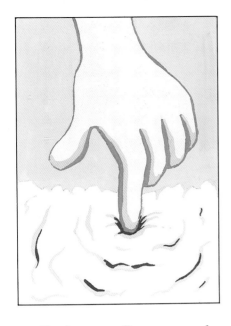
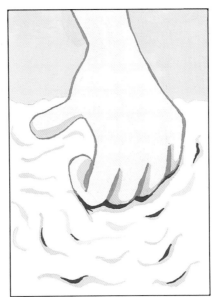
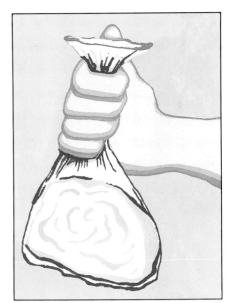

➠ Push your finger gently down on the surface of chop-and-glop. Pull it away.

➠ Put some chop-and-glop in a cup. Try to pour it into another cup.

➠ Roll a round ball of chop-and-glop in your hand. Put it over your

fingers. Watch (and feel) what happens.

➠ Try pounding your fist into chop-and-glop.

➠ Slowly work your finger through chop-and-glop to the bottom of the bowl.

➠ Put some chop-and-glop in a plastic bag.

Move it around in the bag. What happens to its shape?

➠ Hold a ball of chop-and-glop over the sink and drop it.

➠ Add a drop or two of food coloring. Mix with a spoon. What happens to the color?

Let's Experiment!

WHAT TO DO

1. Chop-and-glop is a COLLOID. Colloids are a little like liquids and a little like solids. Some everyday colloids are glue, rubber, plastic, milk, gel, gelatin, and foam. Find as many colloids around your house as you can. Make a list and see how many you can come up with.

2. Choose a few of the colloids in your home to test. Try the same tests with them you tried with chop-and-glop. Write down what happens for each test.

Are all colloids like chop-and-glop? What differences did you find? Can you explain those differences?

WANT TO DO MORE?

➧ Find out what happens if you leave chop-and-glop out in the air for a day or two. What happens if you seal it in a plastic bag without any air? Can you figure out why there is a difference?

➧ Put chop-and-glop in a shallow pan. Add a drop of red food coloring near one end. Put a drop of blue food coloring near the other end. Mix. What happens?

➧ Milk is a colloid that acts like a liquid. Why do you think this is?

➧ Try putting some dry cornstarch into very hot water. What happens?

Handy Hints

☞ Chop-and-glop begins to dry out and get crumbly within an hour or two. If necessary, add a few drops of water. Be careful, not too much. You don't want chop-and-glop soup.

☞ Be careful with food coloring. It stains clothes and furniture.

Why-Oh-Why?

Why do chop-and-glop and the other colloids do the things they do?

Read all about it on page 72.

YOUR NOSE KNOWS

*O*ne famous chef claims he can tell from the smell of baking cookies whether the butter used to make them was fresh. Professional perfume sniffers can recognize hundreds of different scents from rosewood to animal musk. Is your nose that good? Find out what your nose knows.

YOU NEED

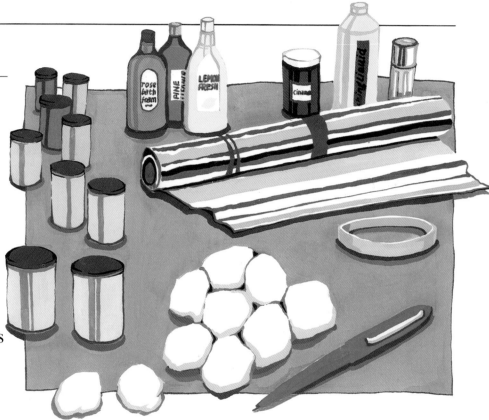

- 8–10 (or more, depending on how many smells you want to use) 35-mm film canisters or small jars with tops
- roll of masking tape
- aluminum foil
- pen
- cotton balls
- assortment of liquids with strong smells (your choice)

WHAT TO DO

1. Choose the smelly things you want to use. You might try cinnamon, vanilla extract, almond extract, perfumes and colognes of various kinds, cleaning products, bath products, or fruit juices.

2. You'll need two jars and two cotton balls for each smell you use. If you are using glass jars, you'll need to hide what's inside, so the color doesn't give the contents away. Cover the insides of the jars with aluminum foil.

3. Put some of the smelly stuff on each of two cotton balls. Put the cotton in the jars and seal them. Repeat this step for each of the smells you use.

4. Put a piece of masking tape on the bottom of each jar. Write a number on one jar and a letter on the other. Repeat this step for each of the smells you use.

Number	Letter	Odor
1	D	Cinnamon
2	A	Pine cleaner
3	E	Rose cologne
4	B	Vanilla
5	C	Vicks VapoRub®

5. Make a secret chart of the numbers and letters you use so you can keep track of what you are doing. See the example above.

6. Hide the numbered jars around the house.

7. Give a friend one of the lettered jars. Let your friend smell what's inside.

Then your friend must find the numbered jar that matches the smell of the lettered one.

8. From your chart, you can tell whether your friend has found the right jar.

9. Let your friend change the numbers and letters on the jars. Then you try.

Let's Experiment!
YOU NEED

➠ set of food colors
➠ cotton balls

WHAT TO DO

1. The object is to find out if our eyes interfere with our noses. Dip cotton balls in a little water mixed with a drop or two of food coloring. Make red, yellow, green, and blue balls. Let them dry.

2. Put different smells on the colors. There's an example on the next page.

Odor	Color 1	Color 2
Old Spice® aftershave	Red	Yellow
Lemon juice	Blue	Red
Almond extract	Green	Blue
Shampoo	Yellow	Green

3. Now mix up the cotton balls and ask your friends to match them by smell. Is it easier with their eyes closed?

Handy Hints

☞ The more smells you use, the more fun the game is.

☞ Smells sealed inside glass jars or film cans will last a long time. Keep your jars or cans in a shoe box and add new smells to your collection as you find them.

☞ Colored solutions, such as gravy flavoring or cola drinks, can color the cotton and give away the secret. Wrap colored cotton balls loosely in plastic wrap, then hide them under white cotton balls in the can or jar. The smell will get through, but the color won't show.

☞ Be careful with food coloring. It can stain your skin and clothes.

WANT TO DO MORE?

➠ "Your Nose Knows" makes a great game for parties. Divide your guests in two groups. Give numbered jars to one group and lettered jars to the other. Have each person find another who is carrying the same smell.

➠ Go outdoors to find new smells. You know about flowers, but some leaves also give off a strong odor when crushed. How does the rain smell? What other smells can you pick out on the street?

Why-Oh-Why?

Your nose knows a lot about the world.

Find out how nose-y you can be by turning to page 73.

WHIRLY-GIGGLE

Look there! High above the city. It's the Radio SCI-6 helicopter reporting traffic jams. Those rotors turn so fast, all you can see is the whirl.

Have you ever thought about what makes those blades turn? A motor turns them, of course. But did you know that the helicopter will spin if the pilot turns the engine off? Try some six-minute science to find out why.

YOU NEED

⟫ pencil
⟫ paper
⟫ paper clips
⟫ scissors

WHAT TO DO

1. Trace the shape of the whirly-giggle onto a piece of paper.

2. Cut out along the outside edges.

3. Follow the numbers, cutting on the solid lines and folding on the dotted lines.

⟫ Cut at 1 and 2.

⟫ Fold under at 3 and 4.

⟫ Fold the end under at 5 and attach a paper clip.

⟫ Cut at 6.

⟫ Fold one arm toward you at 7.

⟫ Fold the other arm away from you at 8.

4. Throw your whirly-giggle as high in the air as you can. Watch it come down.

5. Let your whirly-giggle spin to the ground while you watch it from above. Which way is it spinning?

6. Now fly your whirly-giggle and watch it from underneath. Which way is it spinning now? What changed—you or the whirly-giggle?

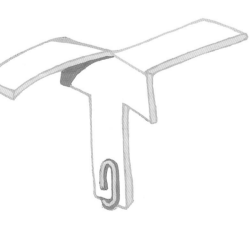

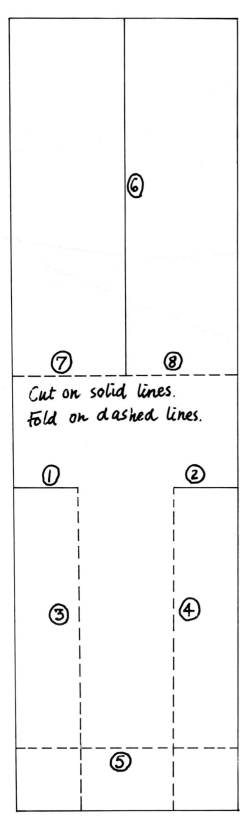

Cut on solid lines.
Fold on dashed lines.

"Whirly - Giggle
Pattern"

Let's Experiment!

WHAT TO DO

1. To make an angel that spins to the ground, trace the shape on the following page onto your paper. Cut it out.

2. Then change one thing at a time until you find a way to make it fly. For example, you might try bending one or both arms or adding paper clips. Keep records of your test flights.

Handy Hints

☞ Lightweight paper flies better than construction paper or cardboard.

☞ Metal paper clips work better than plastic ones.

WANT TO DO MORE?

➡ Maple seeds "fly" the same way the whirly-giggle does. Find some and see.

➡ Do what engineers do—improve on your design. Try making the arms of your whirly-giggle longer or shorter, fatter or thinner. Try changing the length or width of the shaft. Try different amounts of weight. Can you make a whirly-giggle that flies slower, longer, or in a different pattern?

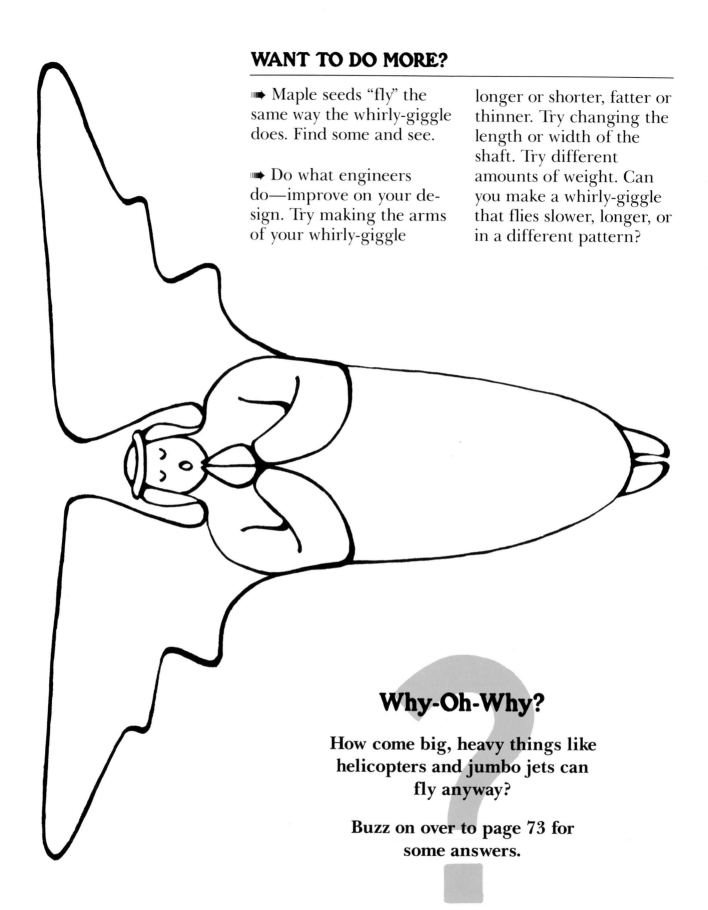

Why-Oh-Why?

How come big, heavy things like helicopters and jumbo jets can fly anyway?

Buzz on over to page 73 for some answers.

30

UNDERCOVER WORK

*P*lant a seed. Wait a week or two. If you're lucky, a plant appears.

   Have you ever wondered what's happening under the ground while you're waiting? Some six-minute gardening will uncover the secrets of the seed.

YOU NEED

- ➡ 1 plastic sandwich bag
- ➡ stapler
- ➡ 4 dried beans or bean seeds
- ➡ masking tape
- ➡ water

WHAT TO DO

1. Soak four dried beans or seeds in water overnight.

2. The next day, put a row of staples through both sides of a plastic sandwich bag. Make the row a little over an inch (3 cm) from the bottom of the bag.

3. Put a little water in the bag. The level of the water should be just below the staples. If the water is too high, it will drip through the staple holes.

4. Put the beans on the staples. Your bag should look like this:

5. Tape the bag to a wall, table edge, or windowsill. Make sure you leave the top of the bag open. Choose a spot where you can watch the bag every day.

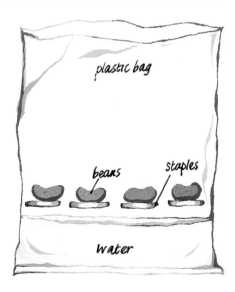

6. Watch what happens in the bag. Make drawings of the changes you see. Add water if the level gets too low.

7. When your beans get big, plant them in pots or outdoors.

Let's Experiment!

YOU NEED

➠ 3 plastic sandwich bags

➠ 12 dried beans or bean seeds

➠ stapler

➠ water

WHAT TO DO

1. Repeat Steps 1, 2 and 3 from page 31.

2. When you put the beans in the bag, turn them in four different directions, like this:

3. Continue as before. Watch carefully. Which appears first—the stem or the root? Do the beans grow upside down? Do they grow sideways? Why do they grow the way they do?

4. Try another experiment. Make two identical bags. Put one in the light and the other in the dark. Do the plants grow the same way? Can you think of a reason why?

WANT TO DO MORE?

➠ Soak a bean and pull it open. You'll see the EMBRYO bean inside. The big, fleshy halves of the bean are called COTYLEDONS, or seed

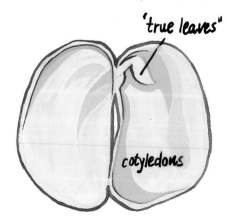

leaves. They give the growing plant its food until the real leaves appear and start to make the plant's food. Do you know where plants get their food? It's not from soil. You've just proved that with your undercover work!

➠ Here's another way to watch seeds sprout. Soak a few beans overnight. Soak some paper towels in water. Put the beans inside a clear plastic cup or glass. Fill the glass with damp towels. Use the paper towels to press the seeds against the sides of the glass. Keep the towels moist. Watch the seeds begin to grow.

➠ Grow some other kinds of seeds this way. Radishes work really well.

Handy Hints

☞ You don't need seeds for this undercover work. Ordinary dried beans that you might cook for dinner work very well—and they're cheap, too.

☞ If you seal your bag closed, the seeds may stay too wet and rot. You'll know rot when you see (and smell!) it. Be sure to leave the bag open so air can get in.

☞ If you forget to keep water in your bag, your seeds may dry out and die. Keep the water level just below the staples.

Why-Oh-Why?

What happens when seeds start to grow?

Where do they get their food?

Why do they grow differently in the light than in the dark?

Why do stems grow up and roots grow down?

Leaf over to page 73 to find out.

V-ROOM, V-ROOM

*R*ace day at the Indy 500. Tension mounts as the cars take their places. The flag drops.

   They're off! Hear the crowd roar! Feel the power, the speed, the excitement!

   What? You say it's not race day and things are pretty quiet around your house? Never mind. You can build a six-minute science race car and stage a race of your own.

YOU NEED

- 1 3″ × 5″ index card
- 2 soda straws
- ruler
- 4 spools
- scissors
- 1 piece of paper
- pencil
- small ball of modeling clay
- transparent tape

WHAT TO DO

1. Center two soda straws over the index card near the ends. Use your ruler to get equal lengths of straw extending on each side. Tape the straws in place.

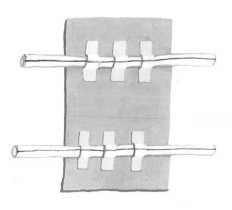

2. Slip a spool over each soda-straw end. Put a knob of modeling clay over the straw ends to keep the spools from falling off.

3. Put your car on a smooth surface and push. It should roll straight and smooth. If it doesn't, you may need to solve some problems. See "Handy Hints" on the next page.

4. Try running your car on a table top and then on a carpet. Which lets your car roll better?

Let's Experiment!

YOU NEED

⟹ tape measure

⟹ masking tape

⟹ watch with second hand or stopwatch

WHAT TO DO

1. Set up a race track for your car. Use a tape measure and masking tape to lay out a test track. Four or five feet (120–150 cm) is a good length. Mark the starting line and the finish line with masking tape.

2. Use a watch with a second hand or a stopwatch to measure how long it takes your car to finish the race.

3. Change the design of your car. Try using larger or smaller spools for wheels. Fold your index card in half and make the straws shorter. Do these changes make your car faster or slower?

4. Make two cars that are exactly the same except for one thing—maybe one has big wheels and the other has little wheels. Race the two cars together. Does the difference affect how fast the car can go? How do you know?

Handy Hints

☞ Pull the paper labels off the ends of your spools. Bits of paper can catch on the clay or cardboard and keep the spool from turning.

☞ The clay knobs on the ends of the straws should be tight enough to keep the spools from wobbling. But don't make them so tight that they stop the spools from turning.

☞ If you are using small spools, you may want to trim your soda straws.

WANT TO DO MORE?

➠ Which rolls best—plastic, wooden, or Styrofoam® spools? Find spools made of different materials and do an experiment to find out.

➠ Try using cardboard wheels instead of spools. What must you do to make them work?

➠ If you want your car to look more like a car, trace this pattern onto paper. Use carbon paper to transfer the design onto two index cards. Color your car shapes and cut them out. Cut two slits about an inch (2.5 cm) long in the base of your car as shown. Insert the tabs into your car base, fold them, and tape them underneath.

Why-Oh-Why?

Why do some cars roll faster than others?

Zoom on over to page 74 to find out.

LEERY LIZARDS

*H*ave you ever seen a purple sandpiper sitting on her nest? How about a sea moth? (It's not a moth. It's a fish.) Have you ever spotted a ptarmigan in the snow or a stick insect on a branch? Chances are, you probably haven't.

If you're like most people, you could walk (or swim) right by these animals and never see them. That's because their colors and shapes blend in with their environment. Scientists say these animals are CAMOUFLAGED.

Soldiers are camouflaged when they dress in clothes spotted with green and brown and black.

How does camouflage help a soldier? Does camouflage help an animal the same way? If you have six minutes, you can find out.

YOU NEED

- 1 piece of white paper for each lizard
- scissors
- pencil
- box of crayons or colored markers
- transparent tape
- bottle of glue (from which a small amount will be used)
- a small amount of natural materials such as twigs or grass that you collect from outdoors
- watch with second hand or stopwatch

WHAT TO DO

1. Meet Leery Lizard. Trace Leery Lizard onto white paper. Trace as many lizards as you want to camouflage.

2. Look around the room or pick a spot outdoors. Where would your Leery Lizards be safe if they were camouflaged?

3. Color your Leery Lizards so that they blend in with some spots in the room or outdoors. If you are playing outside, try gluing leaves, twigs, or grass onto your lizards.

4. Put your lizards in plain sight. It's not fair to hide them under things. Their own camouflage has to protect them against PREDATORS. Predators are animals that eat other animals.

5. Invite a friend to play predator once you have your Leery Lizards in place.

6. Give the predator a short period of time to find as many Leery Lizards as possible. Try one or two minutes, depending on how large the search area is.

Look at the Leery Lizards the predator didn't find. What was good about their camouflage? You can do an experiment to test one difference.

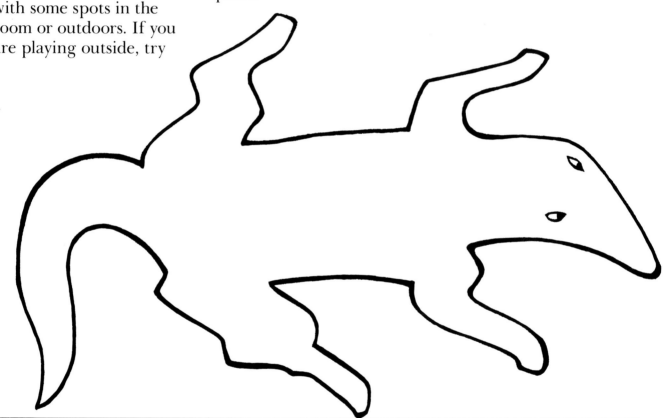

Let's Experiment!

WHAT TO DO

1. Test solid-color lizards on solid-color backgrounds against striped lizards on striped backgrounds. How will you make sure your test is fair? What numbers will you need to prove one kind of camouflage is better than the other?

2. Test solid colors versus patterns. Which fools the eye better? Prove your answer with numbers.

WANT TO DO MORE?

➡ "Leery Lizards" makes a great party game. Give everyone several lizards to color. Let your guests take turns playing predator. Give prizes to the predators who capture the most lizards in one minute.

➡ Invent an animal of your own to camouflage. Try disguising an orange or a lemon. Can your pretend animal escape a sharp-eyed predator?

Handy Hints

☞ You can keep your Leery Lizards from sliding off a tree or a wall. Put a piece of folded tape on the back. Then the tape won't show and give away your Leery Lizard's hiding spot.

☞ Camouflage isn't always a color or pattern. Some Leery Lizards may escape because they hide where predators don't look, even though in full view. Try the sides of bookcases, the backs of chairs, or the legs of tables. Are there any real animals that escape predators this way?

Why-Oh-Why?

How did some animals end up camouflaged?

Why are some so obviously *not* camouflaged?

A few answers appear on page 74.

SEESAW, SWING, AND DRAW

*H*ow about a trip to the playground for some six-minute science? Find someone who's bigger than you. Can the two of you balance on the seesaw? Find someone who's smaller than you. What do you have to do to balance on the seesaw? How is it different?

Find out what makes this balancing act work. Do some experiments on your own.

YOU NEED

→ small lump of modeling clay

→ ruler

→ scissors

→ 1 cereal box

→ coins

Let's Experiment!

WHAT TO DO

1. Cut a V-shaped piece from two sides of a cereal box. (You'll end up with a wedge.)

2. Push two lumps of modeling clay onto a table. (Better ask permission first. Clay can leave spots on good furniture.)

3. Turn the wedge so that the pointed side is up. Push the bottom pieces into the clay. Presto!

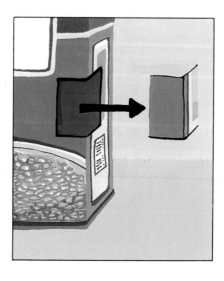

You've made a solid support for your seesaw. It's called a FULCRUM.

4. Balance a ruler on the fulcrum. Where does it balance? (Maybe somewhere near the middle?)

5. Using stacks of coins or lumps of clay, find ways to make equal loads balance. Get six coins that are all alike. Put three on each side. Do they balance? Now get three of a different size coin. Will they balance three of the coins you started with?

6. Try balancing unequal weights when the fulcrum is not under the middle of the ruler. What makes it work?

Are you ready to do more? You can make a simple BALANCE that will let you compare the weights of little things.

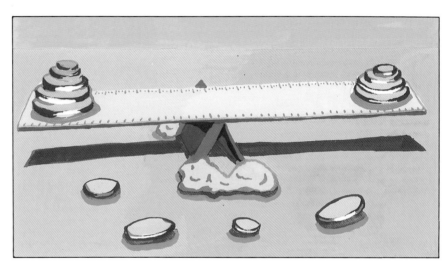

Let's Experiment!

YOU NEED

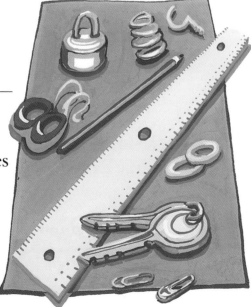

- pencil
- ruler with a hole in the middle and holes at equal distances from the ends
- 2 paper clips
- an assortment of small "junk" items

WHAT TO DO

1. Stick a hunk of clay on a table or counter. (Remember to get permission to put clay on a table, because it can stain.)

2. Stick a pencil into the clay, point side up.

3. Check your ruler. It should have a round hole in the middle. It should have one or two holes at equal distances from the ends. If your ruler isn't right, try to find one that is.

4. Put the point of the pencil through the center hole of the ruler.

5. Bend the paper clips open to make hooks. You'll use these hooks for hanging things from your balance.

6. Hang two little things from the hooks. Which is heavier? How can you tell? Weigh something else. Which is the lightest of the three things you have weighed? Which is the heaviest? How do you know?

WANT TO DO MORE?

➡ Try making a hanging pan balance with your pencil and ruler. Use string to hang paper cups from the ends of the ruler. Put little things in the cups. See which weighs more.

➡ Turn ideas about balancing into designs for model bridges. Try building a swing bridge. Use string and soda straws. Or try making a drawbridge you can pull up whenever an enemy attacks your imaginary castle.

Handy Hints

☞ Don't use weights that are too tall on your ruler. They're hard to balance. Keep your loads low and flat.

☞ Small loads are easier to balance than large ones.

☞ Don't worry about getting a perfect balance that lasts for a long time. Rulers are easy to tip. Just find the spot where things seem to balance best.

Why-Oh-Why?

In the third century B.C., the Greek scientist Archimedes wrote, "Give me where to stand, and I will move the earth." What did he have in mind?

Find out on page 74.

42

IN THE SWING

How are grandfather clocks and swings in the playground alike? Look at how they are made. The swing is a weight suspended from above. So is the pendulum in the clock. What makes them swing fast or slow? Do some six-minute science to find out.

YOU NEED

- ▶ scissors
- ▶ string
- ▶ 5 large metal washers
- ▶ transparent tape
- ▶ ruler
- ▶ watch with second hand or stopwatch

Let's Experiment!

WHAT TO DO

1. Cut a piece of string 12 inches (30 cm) long. Tie a washer to the end of the string.

2. Tape the other end of the string to the edge of a table, leaving a little string above the tape.

3. You've made a PENDULUM. Pull back on the washer and let go. Watch

your pendulum swing. It should swing freely without hitting anything.

4. Start your pendulum swinging. Count how many times it swings in 15 seconds.

5. Measure the length of your string from the bottom edge of the table to the knot that holds the

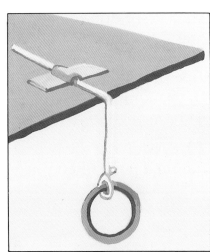

washer. Write down that number.

6. Tie another washer onto the same string (see drawing #2). Tape your pendulum to the table again. Make sure the length of the string is the same as before. If your knot has made your string shorter, let down some string from the top.

7. Time your pendulum swings again. How many times does the pendulum swing in 15 seconds? Does more weight slow the pendulum down? (If you think it does, better try the experiment again.)

8. Tie three, four, even five washers on the string. Make sure you keep the length of the string the same each time you count the number of swings in 15 seconds. If weight does not slow a pendulum down, what does?

9. Try starting the pendulum at higher or lower angles (see drawings #3 and #4). Again, count the swings for 15 seconds. Does it matter how high the pendulum is when it starts swinging?

10. Try giving the pendulum a push when you

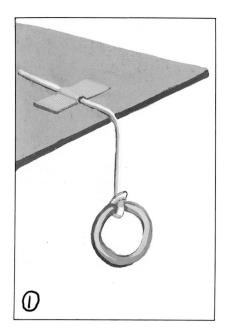

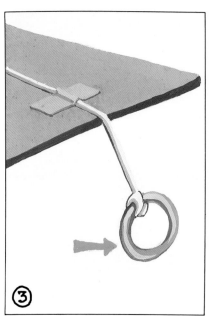

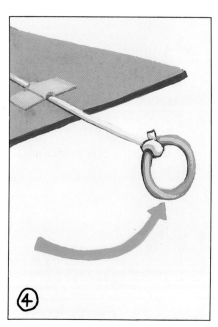

start it. Then try letting it go without a push. Does the push make any difference in how many times it swings in 15 seconds?

11. Cut a 6-inch (15 cm) long piece of string and

an 18-inch (45 cm) long piece of string. Make pendulums with one washer on each string. Count the number of swings in 15 seconds. Does the length of the string make a difference?

WANT TO DO MORE?

➡ Once you know how many times a pendulum swings in 15 seconds, you can use it as a clock. How will you do it? What will you time?

➡ Make two pendulums—one that swings exactly twice as fast as the other. Now make a third pendulum. Make it swing half as fast as the slower one. How could you make it swing one-third as fast? One-fourth?

➡ Cut pictures of pendulum clocks out of catalogs. Predict how fast their pendulums will swing based on what you know now.

Handy Hints

☞ If you don't have washers, any small object with a hole will do. Try curtain rings, Lifesavers®, even small doughnuts. Make weights of your own by baking modeling dough (see "Dough, Dough, Mold, and Go").

☞ You could count one trip out and back as one swing, or the trip out as one swing and the trip back as a second. It doesn't matter, as long as you count the same way every time.

☞ The pendulum may not always swing straight. That's okay, as long as it doesn't get tangled or hit something.

Why-Oh-Why?

What makes pendulums swing faster or slower?

Why does the pendulum eventually stop?

Swing on over to page 75 for the answers.

I'VE GOT RHYTHM, YOU'VE GOT RHYTHM

Centuries ago, people thought that the heart was the organ that caused us to feel love. Today, we believe love is an emotion centered a good deal higher up.

The heart may not love, but it has an even more important job to do. By pumping blood, the heart supplies oxygen to every part of your body. The tiny cells you are made of need a constant supply of oxygen to stay alive.

The human heart beats almost three billion times in a lifetime. That's a three with nine zeros after it!

The heart pumps about 1⅓ gallons (5 l) of blood every minute. That's about the same amount as two six-packs of soda. In a day, that's over 3,000 six-packs!

Would you like to hear your heart beat?

YOU NEED

▷ 1 plastic bottle
▷ small ball of modeling clay

▷ 2 pieces of plastic airline tubing (from an aquarium store), each 16 inches (40 cm) long

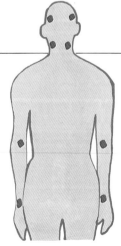

WHAT TO DO

1. Have you ever had a doctor or nurse take your pulse? You can feel your pulse at your wrist, neck, temple, and inside your elbow. Press your first two fingers against your skin.

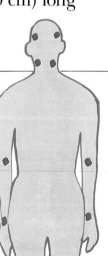

You'll probably feel a gentle throbbing.

2. Find a friend's pulse. Try to feel the throbbing at the wrist, neck, temple, or inside the elbow.

3. Doctors use a tool called a STETHOSCOPE to help them hear the heartbeat. You can make a stethoscope that works almost as well.

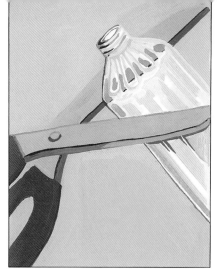

4. Ask an adult to cut the top off a plastic bottle for you, as shown.

5. Put the two pieces of plastic air-line tubing through the mouth of the bottle. Pack modeling clay around the tubes to hold them in place, like this:

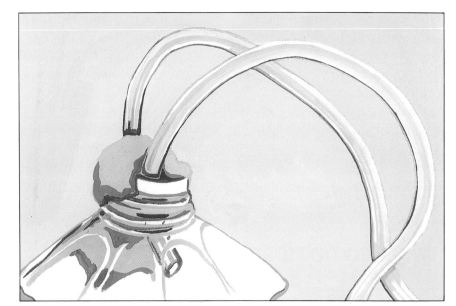

6. Place the wide part of the bottle against your chest. Put the ends of the tubes in your ears. Listen for the steady "lub-dub" sound of your heart.

7. Use your stethoscope to listen to a friend's heart. Now you are ready to experiment.

Let's Experiment!

YOU NEED

➤ watch with second hand or stopwatch

➤ step about 12–16 inches (30–40 cm) high—may be a step on stairs or a sturdy box

WHAT TO DO

1. Take the Harvard Step Test to see how quickly your heart gets back to normal after exercise. First, find your pulse. Count the beats of your heart for 30 seconds. Write this number on a piece of paper. It is your RESTING RATE.

2. Now, see what exercise does to your pulse rate.

Start stepping up and down on a step. Step up with your right foot. Bring the left up beside it. Now step backwards with your right foot to the ground. Bring your left foot down beside your right. Do this once every two seconds (30 times a minute) for five minutes.

3. As soon as you stop, take your pulse for 30 seconds. Write the number down.

4. Wait 30 seconds. Count your pulse again for 30 seconds.

5. Keep doing this until

Handy Hints

☞ Never take someone else's pulse with your thumb. You'll end up counting your own pulse.

☞ Sometimes when your head is on a pillow, you can hear your pulse quite clearly. Keep a stopwatch ready beside your bed so you can count the beats.

☞ Don't let anyone else use your stethoscope. Germs on the plastic tubing can spread ear infections.

☞ If you have trouble hearing your heart beat, try moving your stethoscope to different places on your chest. Just to the left of center is usually best. Be very quiet and listen closely. The sound is not loud.

your pulse rate drops to your resting rate. How many minutes did you need? If you needed more than a minute or two, you may need to get more exercise to keep your heart healthy.

WANT TO DO MORE?

In general, the smaller the animal, the faster the heartbeat. Look up the heart rates of animals.

Here are a few to get you started: (They're all the number of heartbeats in a minute.)

➡ hedgehog (hibernating)	3
➡ frog (freezing weather)	8
➡ elephant	20
➡ ox	25
➡ frog (warm weather)	30
➡ human adult	70
➡ human baby	130
➡ rabbit	200
➡ hedgehog (active)	250
➡ mouse	500

Athletes who are in excellent physical condition usually have much slower heartbeats than people who are less active. Find out why.

When you were little, your heart beat much faster than it does now. Women's hearts generally beat faster than men's for the same reason. Can you guess what it is?

Why-Oh-Why?

What keeps your heart beating?

What makes it speed up when you exercise?

Why do athletes have slower heart rates than couch potatoes?

Get to the heart of the matter on page 76.

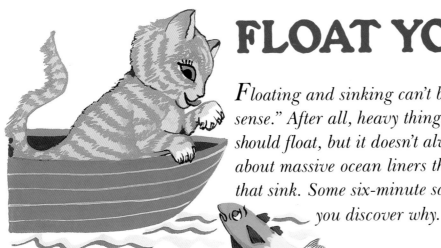

FLOAT YOUR BOAT

Floating and sinking can't be explained using "common sense." After all, heavy things should sink and light things should float, but it doesn't always work that way. Think about massive ocean liners that float and tiny little marbles that sink. Some six-minute science experiments will help you discover why.

YOU NEED

- small ball of modeling clay
- sink or pan filled with water
- paper towels

Let's Experiment!

WHAT TO DO

1. Roll the clay into a ball and put it in the water. What happens?

2. Remove the clay from the water and dry it off with a paper towel.

3. Now, change the clay in some way so that it will float. (You're on your own to figure out how.)

4. Once you make your clay float, look at what you have done. Have you changed the weight of the clay? Is it lighter now than it was before? If not, what *is* different?

Let's Experiment!

YOU NEED

⟫ 20 or more coins

⟫ small ball of modeling clay

⟫ sink or pan filled with water

⟫ paper towels

WANT TO DO MORE?

➡ When you change the shape of the clay, you don't change its weight. You change its VOLUME. That's the amount of space something takes. (See "A Pound of Feathers and a Pound of Lead.") Float a piece of aluminum foil and then sink it just by changing its volume.

Why-Oh-Why?

Why do some heavy things float and some light things sink?

Row on over to page 76 to find out.

WHAT TO DO

1. Make your clay float.

2. Stack coins on your clay. How many will it hold before it sinks?

3. Remove your clay from the water and dry it with a paper towel.

4. Now, change the clay in some way. Can you make it hold more coins? Do some changes make it hold fewer coins before it sinks?

5. Make a chart showing the different things you've tried with your clay and how many coins it held each time.

Handy Hints

☞ Clay that's too wet is hard to work with. Dry your clay with a paper towel each time you take it out of the water.

☞ Use coins that are all the same denomination so that you add an equal amount of weight each time you test your clay.

☞ The way you stack the coins can make a difference. Why should you do it the same way each time you test your clay.

A POUND OF FEATHERS AND A POUND OF LEAD

*F*ool a friend with a trick question. Which is harder to carry—a pound of feathers or a pound of lead? Do you get the joke? They weigh the same, so one is as easy to carry as the other. But something's different. What is it?

It's easy to pick things up and tell if they are heavy or light. But have you ever thought about how much space things take up? A pound of feathers weighs the same as a pound of lead. The difference is how much space the feathers take.

The amount of space something takes up is called its VOLUME.

It's easy to see different volumes in your cereal bowl. Some six-minute science will show you how.

YOU NEED

- diet scale
- 3 or more boxes of different types of cereal
- 3 or more cereal bowls of the same type
- 3 or more clear plastic or glass tumblers or jars

WHAT TO DO

1. Read the labels on the cereal boxes. How much is one serving? (Usually one ounce [28 g], but some say more or less.)

2. Weigh one ounce (28 g) of some cereal. Use the diet scale. (If you don't have a diet scale, build the cup balance described on page 42. Then weigh equal amounts of two cereals in the cups.)

3. Put the cereal in a bowl. Does it look like a lot or a little?

4. Weigh one ounce (28 g) of another cereal.

5. Put it in another bowl. Does it look like more than the first one? Less?

The same?

6. Try one or two more cereals. Compare their volumes. Remember, they all weigh the same.

7. Put each cereal in a tall, clear glass or jar. (If your jars are short, weigh

½ ounce [14 g] of each cereal.)

8. Put the glasses side by side. What differences can you see? Can you explain this puzzle? These things all weigh the same. Their volumes are different.

Let's Experiment!

YOU NEED

⟹ diet scale
⟹ 3 or more boxes of different types of cereal
⟹ paper towels
⟹ measuring cup

WHAT TO DO

1. Weigh the measuring cup on the scale. Record its weight. (If the cup is too heavy for your scale, place a paper towel on the scale. Can you record its weight?)

2. Measure ½ cup of one cereal. Weigh the cup and the cereal. (Or weigh the cereal on the paper towel.) Subtract the weight of the cup (or the weight of the paper towel) to find the weight of the cereal.

3. Repeat Step 2 with several other cereals.

4. Make a table. What does the table tell you? How can you explain your results? Can you say you have more of one cereal than another if you measured a half cup of each?

① Name of cereal	② Volume of cereal	③ Weight of empty cup	④ Weight of cup with cereal	⑤ Weight of cereal (subtract column 3 from column 4)
Rice pops	½ cup			
Cornflakes	½ cup			
Bran flakes	½ cup			
Weetos	½ cup			
Sugar puffs	½ cup			

WANT TO DO MORE?

➠ Crush the cereals into crumbs. Use a potato masher or a heavy can. Then compare volumes. What happens when you push the air out?

➠ Look around your house for some items that have equal volume but different weights. For example, a full bottle and an empty bottle take up the same amount of space. Do they weigh the same?

➠ Find some things that float in water. Find some that sink. Find some surprises—heavy things that float and light things that sink. Why does this happen? (See "Float Your Boat" for a clue.)

➠ Find a small cardboard box. Fill it with rocks or sand. Hold the box and stand on the bathroom scale. What do you weigh? Now fill the box with cotton balls or Styrofoam® packing pieces. What do you weigh now? Has the weight of the box changed? Has the volume?

Handy Hints

☞ Use Grape-Nuts® cereal and puffed rice or wheat to see big differences.

☞ Be sure your scale reads zero before you start.

Why-Oh-Why?

How can things that weigh the same have different volumes?

How can things that take up the same amount of space not weigh the same?

Turn to page 76 to find out.

LIGHT, LIGHT, BURNING BRIGHT

Pop a battery in a flashlight and off you go, confident you can explore the dark. But stop a minute. Have you ever thought about how and why that flashlight works?

Let's Experiment!

YOU NEED

⇒ 1 empty shallow can, such as a tuna can

⇒ 4 "D" batteries

⇒ set of miniature Christmas tree lights

⇒ masking tape

⇒ aluminum foil

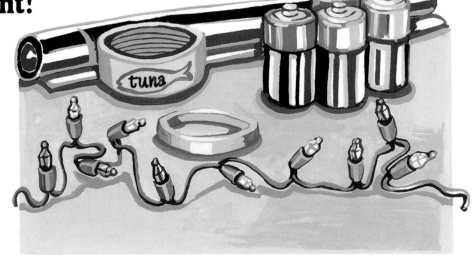

WHAT TO DO

Important safety warnings: Do not plug anything into a wall socket during this experiment. You will use batteries to light your lights.
Do not cut the lights apart yourself. Ask an adult for help.

1. Ask an adult to help you cut some lights and wire from a set of miniature Christmas tree lights.

2. Ask an adult to help you trim the plastic insulation away from the ends of the wires to expose the copper wire underneath. Your lights should look like this:

3. Get a clean, dry, shallow can (the kind tuna comes in) or a similar container.

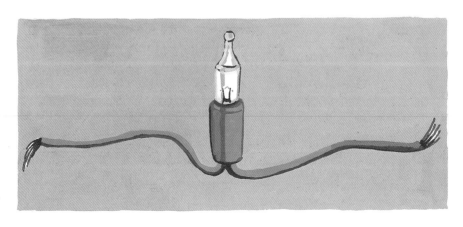

4. Push several layers of crumpled aluminum foil into the bottom of the can.

5. Look at your batteries. Notice that each has a flat end marked − and a pointed end marked +.

6. Place the four batteries in the can. Stand the − end up on two of the batteries. Stand the + end up on the other two.

7. Touch one end of your light wire to one end of a battery. Now touch the other end to another battery. Does the bulb light? If not, try another battery.

8. Which two ends must touch the wire to make the bulb light?

Let's Experiment!

YOU NEED

- ➤ 1 tall can, the kind soups or canned vegetables come in
- ➤ 4 "D" batteries
- ➤ set of miniature Christmas tree lights
- ➤ masking tape
- ➤ aluminum foil

WHAT TO DO

1. Still working with your tuna can, turn all the − ends of the batteries down in the can. Will the bulb light?

2. Turn all the + ends down in the can. Will the bulb light?

3. Turn one of the + ends up in the can? Will the bulb light?

4. Turn three of the + ends up in the can. What must you do to make the bulb light?

5. Now set up your tall can. Put aluminum foil in the bottom. Use the kind of can soups or canned vegetables come in.

6. Stack the batteries inside on top of each other, as shown. How must the + and − ends of the batteries be turned to make the bulb light?

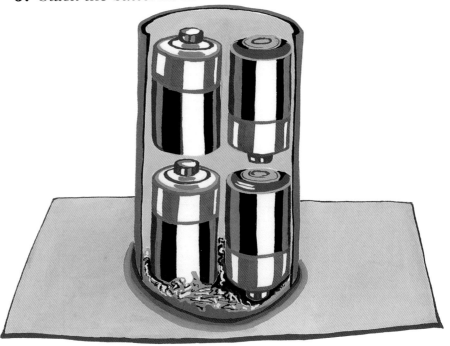

Handy Hints

☞ You can use old strings of lights that have been thrown away. It's probably not the whole set that's bad, just a few bulbs. Try the bulbs until you find one that lights.

☞ If you want to keep a light burning, tape the wire to the battery with masking tape. Don't leave it taped too long. Batteries run down, and lights burn out.

WANT TO DO MORE?

⮕ Make a question and answer game. Write questions in a column on a piece of cardboard. Write answers in another column. Punch a hole beside each question and each answer. Put a brass paper fastener in each hole. On the back of the cardboard, wire the correct answer to its question, as shown.

⮕ Make a tester by taping wire and a light to a battery like this:

⮕ Touch the ends of the tester to the brass fasteners. The bulb will light only for correct answers.

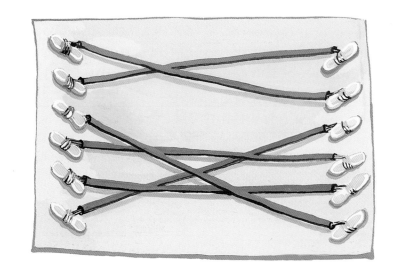

Why-Oh-Why?

How can batteries cause lights to glow?

Why do some hookups work and others not?

Turn to page 77 to cast some light on the situation.

DYEING TO TRY IT

In the year 2006, synthetic dyeing will be 150 years old. Dyeing is how we get color into fabrics, paper, and other materials. Synthetic means human-made. Before people learned how to make dyes, they got colors from materials in nature, especially plants.

Do some six-minute science experiments, and you can get dyes from plants, too.

Let's Experiment!

YOU NEED

➡ 1 safety pin

➡ 1 piece of white cotton fabric or white yarn

➡ assortment of natural materials to use for dyeing (flowers and leaves, onion skins, walnut shells, purple grape juice, etc.)

➡ 4 teaspoons of alum

➡ 1 teaspoon cream of tartar

➡ pot

➡ stove

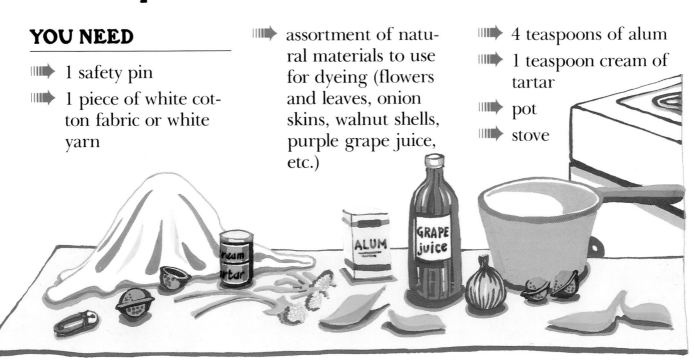

WHAT TO DO

Caution: You need an adult to help you with the cooking. Do not try to use the stove on your own.
Caution: If you pick flowers or collect leaves in meadows, forests, or parks, you may kill a rare or valuable plant or rob an animal of its home and food. You may also spoil someone's hard work and ruin the beauty of the park for visitors.

Pick flowers and leaves only in a place where you have permission.

1. Just about any weed, leaf or flower will give you

some kind of color, but it may not always be the one you expect. If you can't get weeds or leaves, try natural dye sources from the kitchen: onion skins, fruit or vegetable juices, berries, or other strongly colored plant material.

2. In this experiment, you will compare the effect of a MORDANT (a chemical that fixes, or sets, a dye) on the color your dye produces. Divide your white yarn or cotton fabric into two equal amounts. Put a safety pin in one piece.

3. You'll need to use the stove for this part, so *get an adult to help.* Add four teaspoons of alum and one teaspoon of cream of tartar to about a quart (.95 l) of water in a saucepan. Add the piece of white cotton fabric or yarn with the safety pin in it to the pot. Bring to a boil. Turn down the heat and simmer for one hour. Don't do anything to the other half of your fabric or yarn.

4. After the simmering time is over, cool and rinse your cloth or yarn. Let it dry before dyeing.

5. On another day, pick out what you want to use to get dye from. Onion skins are good to start with. Put some onion skins in a pan with only enough water to cover both pieces of the fabric or yarn you want to dye. *Now get an adult to help.* Put the pan on the stove and simmer for 10 or 15 minutes. If the color isn't bright, cook for 5 or 10 minutes longer. Cool. Rinse and dry.

6. After your dyed material dries, compare the one that was treated with the mordant (it has the safety pin in it) with the one that was not treated. Can you see any difference in the color?

7. Leave the dyed pieces in strong sunlight for a few days. Does the mordant make a difference in how long the color lasts?

WANT TO DO MORE?

➠ Native Americans made beautiful wall hangings showing the colors they got from the plants around them. You can make one, too. It might look something like this:

Handy Hints

☞ You can buy cream of tartar in the spice section at the supermarket. If your supermarket doesn't carry alum, you will probably find it at a pharmacy. Ask for alum if it is hard to find.

☞ Old white T-shirts are great for experiments with dyeing. Just cut them up into strips or blocks.

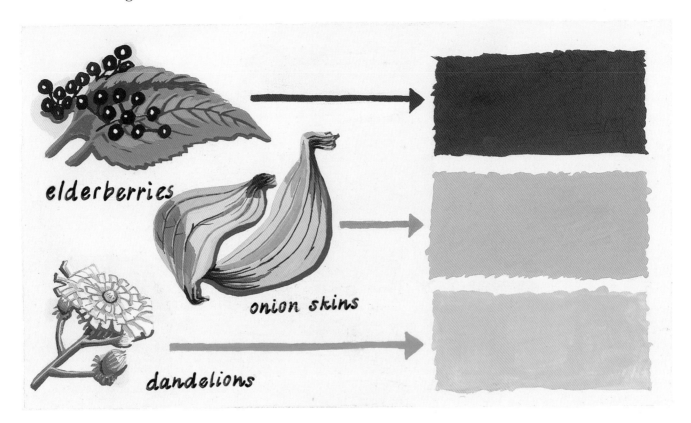

elderberries

onion skins

dandelions

Why-Oh-Why?

How do dyes work?

What difference does a mordant make?

Turn to page 78 for the end of this vivid tale.

AND THE MUSIC GOES ROUND AND ROUND

Want to make music, but you have no instruments to play? Build your own and figure out how they work.

Let's Experiment!

YOU NEED

▶ 2 plastic mixing bowls of same size and shape

▶ 6 bulldog clips

▶ 6 or more rubber bands of varying thicknesses

WHAT TO DO

1. Place two bulldog clips on a rubber band, like this:

2. Attach one clip to the rim of a bowl.

3. Stretch the rubber band to the other side of the bowl and attach the other clip to the rim. Make sure your clips and bands are straight and even, like this:

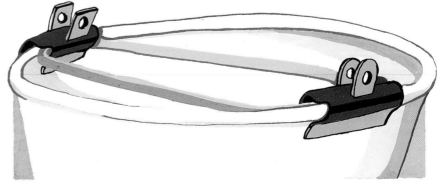

4. Pluck the two segments of rubber band as if they were the strings of a guitar. Are they the same PITCH (highness or lowness)? If not, adjust them until their pitch sounds the same.

5. Repeat Steps 1–4 with

the other bowl and a rubber band that is thicker or thinner than the first one you used. Make sure both rubber bands are stretched the same length.

6. Pluck both sets of strings. Which one has a higher pitch?

7. Now, thread another clip over one of the lengths of rubber band. Stretch to the rim of the bowl and attach the clip in an off-center position as shown. You should have three different lengths of rubber band now. Which has the highest pitch? Which has the lowest?

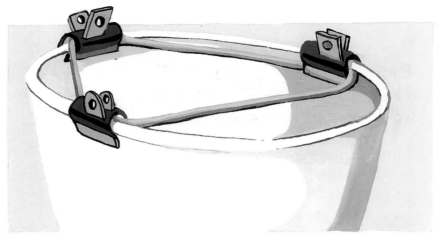

8. Try the same thing with your other bowl and other rubber band. How does changing the length of the band affect the pitch?

9. Working with one bowl at a time, leave the clips in place. While plucking a section of the rubber band with one hand, use the other to pull the band tighter. Do that by stretching from the outside of the bulldog clip, as shown.

10. Listen as you pluck and stretch. What happens to the pitch?

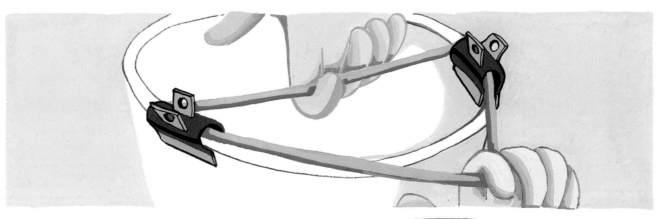

WANT TO DO MORE?

➡ Select another rubber band, one that is longer or shorter than the one you used before. Run the new band around the *tops* of the clips, like this:

Pluck the top band and the bottom one. Are the bands the same pitch? Can you think of two reasons

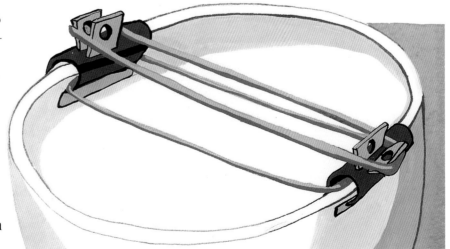

why not? Test your idea by using rubber bands of the same length and thickness.

➠ Use more clips and more rubber bands of different thicknesses. Position rubber bands and clips all around the bowl rim to make an instrument that will play many different notes. How can you adjust the bands to give you the notes you need to play a simple tune?

➠ Build a twelve-string "guitar." You need an empty cardboard box (the kind cake mix comes in works well) and 12 rubber bands, all of different sizes. Open one end of the box and turn the flaps in. Stretch the rubber bands around the length of the box, as shown. Pluck the strings over the open end. What pitch do they make? Move the rubber bands around until you have them in order from the lowest to the highest pitch. What tune can you play on your twelve-string?

Handy Hints

☞ When hooking rubber bands around the tops of the clips, go around the outsides (not the insides). The bands and clips are less likely to slip.

☞ Ask your family to save rubber bands until you have a good selection of different sizes.

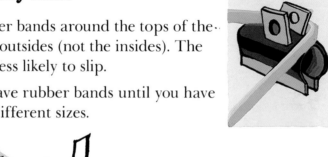

Why-Oh-Why?

What makes sound?

What makes pitch higher or lower?

Face the music and tune into some answers on page 78.

BABY, IT'S COLD OUTSIDE

"Brrr!" said Sinuous Snake. *"It's too cold for sidewinding, and that's a fact."*

"You think so?" asked Rotund Rabbit, munching on a carrot. *"I hadn't noticed. I am* terribly *sleepy, though."*

Both the snake and the rabbit will nap through most of the winter, but the rabbit has two ways of keeping warm that the snake missed out on. Do some six-minute science to find out what they are.

Let's Experiment!

YOU NEED

▸ sink or bucket filled with cold water

▸ 2 large plastic bags

▸ 2 rubber bands

▸ 1 glove or mitten

WHAT TO DO

1. Fill the bucket or sink with cold water.

2. Keeping your hands spread open, pull the bags over your hands.

3. Get someone to help you seal the bags tight with rubber bands at the wrists.

4. Form a fist with one hand. Keep the other hand spread open. Put both hands in the cold water.

5. Which hand feels cold first? (Pay particular attention to your palm.)

6. Repeat the experiment, but this time hold

both hands open. Cover one hand with a glove or mitten. Now, fit plastic bags on both hands. Put your hands in the cold water again. Which hand feels warm longer?

⇒ The way you held your hand and whether you wore a mitten made a difference in how cold your palm felt. What do these experiments have to do with the rabbit and the snake?

⇒ Gloves for kids and fur for rabbits help keep them warm. Can they keep things cold, too?

Handy Hints

☞ Keep the tops of the bags out of the water. Rubber bands can leak, and cold water on your wrists can distract you from the experiment.

☞ Use the smallest bags that will fit over your hands comfortably. And don't forget, the two bags must be identical. Do you know why?

Let's Experiment!

YOU NEED

⇒ 3 plastic cups, all same size and shape

⇒ aluminum foil

⇒ 1 muffler, scarf, coat or other piece of winter clothing

⇒ 3 ice cubes

⇒ clock

⇒ 3 measuring cups

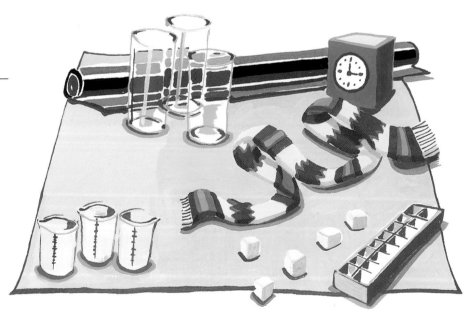

WHAT TO DO

1. Remove three ice cubes from the freezer.

2. Place one in each plastic cup.

3. Leave one cup open to the air.

4. Wrap the second in aluminum foil.

5. Wrap the third in a woolly scarf, coat, or some other piece of winter clothing.

6. Watch the clock and the ice cube that isn't wrapped. When the first cube is nearly all melted, unwrap the other two.

7. Place each cube in a measuring cup. Allow each to melt completely.

8. Read the amount of water that was left in each ice cube. What differences can you spot? Can you explain them?

WANT TO DO MORE?

➡ Compare many different materials to see which makes ice last longest. You might try plastic wrap, silk, cotton, wax paper, construction paper, even an old sock!

➡ If you can locate a thermometer for liquids (not the fever kind), you can compare how materials can help liquids stay warm. Fill three or more glasses with hot water. Record the temperature. Wrap the glasses in materials of your choice, then wait a while and record the temperature again. Do some of the liquids stay hotter than others? Why must you leave one glass unwrapped?

Handy Hints

☞ Make sure you select three ice cubes that are the same size and shape. Broken pieces won't do.

☞ You can shorten the experiment by measuring the amount of water that has melted, rather than the amount still in the cubes. Will this change how you think about your results?

Why-Oh-Why?

Ice cubes and cups of tea may look as if they're sitting still, but they are really speeding and spinning. It's motion that makes ice cubes cold and hot tea hot. Out in the cold for an explanation?

Turn to page 78 and warm up to the idea.

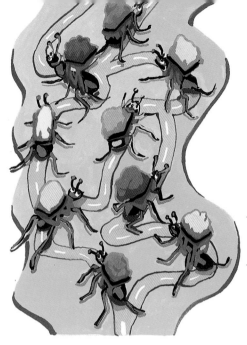

ENZYMES

*L*iving things are made up of cells—millions and millions of cells. Cells are tiny chemical factories. These factories do everything necessary for life—from getting energy from food to getting rid of waste products.

ENZYMES are important workers in these chemical factories. You can't see enzymes, but you can sometimes see what they do. For example, one enzyme in potatoes causes bubbles to be released from hydrogen peroxide. Want to find out what this enzyme needs to do its job best?

Let's Experiment!

YOU NEED

- hydrogen peroxide
- hot water
- cold water
- measuring cup
- 3 clear glasses or plastic cups
- 1 potato
- grater
- set of measuring spoons
- 1 shallow bowl
- 1 spoon
- freezer
- metric ruler

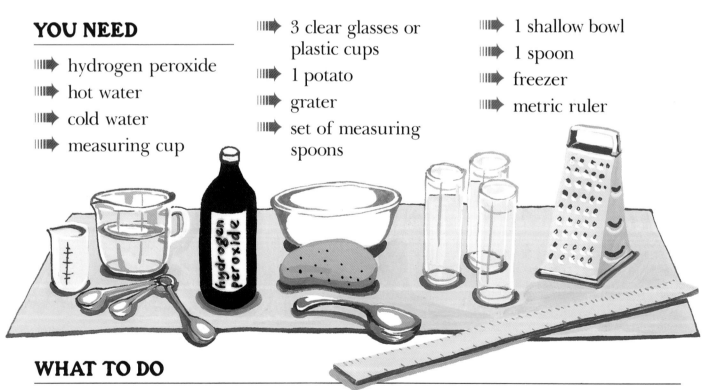

WHAT TO DO

Caution: Hydrogen peroxide is a poison. Do not get it in your eyes or mouth. Do not use peroxide without permission from an adult.
Caution: It is easy to scrape
your fingers when using a grater. Ask an adult for help.

1. Does temperature affect how well the potato enzyme works? To find out, measure ¼ cup

(60 ml) of hydrogen peroxide into a plastic glass. Place it in the freezer. Wait 30 minutes or longer before you go on with the experiment.

2. Measure another ¼ cup (60 ml) of hydrogen peroxide and pour it into another glass. Leave this one at room temperature.

3. Run some very hot water into a shallow bowl. Place the third glass in the bowl. (Make sure the water doesn't rise so high that it spills over into the glass.) Put ¼ cup (60 ml) of hydrogen peroxide in the glass. The water will warm it.

4. Peel and grate the potato finely. (Watch your fingers!)

5. Add a teaspoon of grated potato to each glass. Stir with a spoon. Watch what happens.

6. Wait about five minutes, then measure the height of the foam that collects on the top of the liquid. What differences can you see? Can you explain them?

So the Enzymes can't bubble much when they're cold. What does being warm do? What happens when the enzymes are hungry? Are you ready to find out?

Handy Hints

☞ The more accurate your measurements, the better the results. Pack grated potato so that it is level in the measuring spoon.

☞ Differences in the height of the bubbles will be more obvious if you measure in millimeters. If you don't have a metric rule, trace this ruler onto paper, then paste it onto cardboard.

☞ If you don't get very many bubbles, try using two teaspoons of potato instead of one.

Let's Experiment!

YOU NEED

⟶ measuring cup

⟶ water

⟶ hydrogen peroxide

⟶ 3 teaspoons vinegar

⟶ 5 clear glasses or plastic cups

⟶ set of measuring spoons

⟶ 1 potato

⟶ grater

WHAT TO DO

1. Measure ¼ cup (60 ml) of water into each of five glasses.

2. Add water and hydrogen peroxide to the glasses in these amounts:
Glass 1: 4 tablespoons water
Glass 2: 3 tablespoons water, 1 tablespoon hydrogen peroxide
Glass 3: 2 tablespoons water, 2 tablespoons hydrogen peroxide
Glass 4: 1 tablespoon water, 3 tablespoons hydrogen peroxide
Glass 5: 4 tablespoons hydrogen peroxide

3. Add one teaspoon of grated potato to each glass. Stir.

4. Wait about five minutes. Measure the foam along the side of the glasses as before. Can you explain the difference?

So the Enzymes can't make bubbles very fast if they don't have enough hydrogen peroxide to work on. But what if there's plenty of hydrogen peroxide, but something interferes? Are you ready to find out?

Let's Experiment!

YOU NEED

⟶ water

⟶ measuring cup

⟶ baking soda

⟶ hydrogen peroxide

⟶ masking tape

⟶ 3 glasses or clear plastic cups

⟶ 3 teaspoons vinegar

⟶ 1 potato

⟶ grater

⟶ set of measuring spoons

WHAT TO DO

1. Dissolve 2 teaspoons of baking soda in ¼ cup (60 ml) of water. Set aside.

2. Measure ¼ cup (60 ml) of hydrogen peroxide into each of three glasses. On 3 pieces of masking tape, write the numbers 1, 2, and 3. Stick one piece of tape to each glass.

3. Add 3 teaspoons of water to Glass 1.

4. Add the vinegar to Glass 2.

5. Add 3 teaspoons of the baking soda in water mixture, which you set aside in Step 1, to Glass 3.

6. Add a teaspoon of grated potato to each glass. Stir.

7. After about five minutes, measure the height of the foam that forms along the side of the glasses, as you did before. Can you explain the differences?

WANT TO DO MORE?

➠ Find the smallest amount of vinegar or baking soda you can add without slowing down the bubble making. Find the least amount of hydrogen peroxide you can add to water and still get the enzymes to work.

➠ Dream up your own experiment to see if the amount of potato you use affects the height of the bubbles in the glasses.

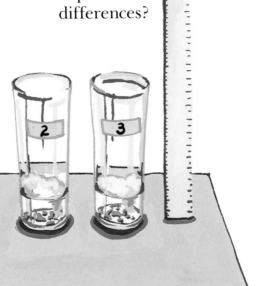

Why-Oh-Why?

How do the enzymes make bubbles?

What speeds them up or slows them down?

Turn to page 78 to find out.

Why-Oh-Why?

The Science Behind Six-Minute Science Experiments

Berry, Berry, Not So Contrary

Chemists call water H_2O (read H-two-oh). That means every water MOLECULE has two hydrogen ATOMS hooked to one oxygen atom. The atoms

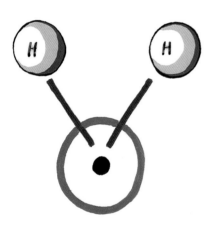

don't stay together all the time. Single hydrogen atoms sometimes float around by themselves. When they break away from the water molecule, they leave an ELECTRON behind. (An electron is a particle that spins around the NUCLEUS of an atom. It always has a negative charge.) Once a nega-

tively charged electron breaks away from a hydrogen atom, the hydrogen atom is left with a positive charge (H^+).

In the same way, some oxygen atoms float around attached to a single hydrogen atom. They have an extra electron and carry a negative charge (OH^-).

Liquids that have more H^+ than OH^- are acid. The more H^+ atoms, the stronger the acid. When the number of OH^- is greater than the number of H^+, the liquid is a base. The more OH^-, the stronger the base. Pure water has the same number of H^+ and OH^-. It is neither an acid nor a base. Pure water is NEUTRAL.

Indicators change colors because the H^+ or OH^- change the shape of the indicator molecule. There are many different kinds of indicators. Some can tell a stronger acid from a weaker one. Some can tell a stronger base from a weaker one.

When an acid and a base combine, the H^+ and the OH^- join to make water. The REACTION releases a gas (carbon dioxide) and some energy. That's why you get mounds of frothy bubbles when you mix vinegar (an acid) with baking soda (a base).

When Is Oh-Two Not Oh-Too?

When vinegar and baking soda react, they release a gas made of one carbon atom and two oxygen atoms. Scientists call this gas carbon dioxide or CO_2.

Yeast contains an ENZYME called catalase. Enzymes are chemicals produced by living things. They make chemical reactions go faster than they would under ordinary conditions.

Hydrogen peroxide is a molecule made of two hydrogen atoms and two oxygen atoms (H_2O_2). It's a lot like a water molecule with an extra oxygen atom attached. Because the bond between the atoms is weak, the extra oxygen atom will break away even at ordinary temperatures —but so slowly you'd never notice. Catalase from the yeast speeds things up enough that you can see bubbles of oxygen gas (O_2) coming out of the hydrogen peroxide. They rise and inflate the balloon.

Yeast are living creatures that have a few tricks to perform. One of their feats is fermentation. They can change sugar into alcohol. That's how beer, wine, and spirits are made. In the process, carbon dioxide gas (CO_2) is given off.

So baking soda and vinegar yield the same gas as sugar and yeast, but by very different chemical processes.

Tightrope Walker

The trick in balancing on a tightrope is to position the CENTER OF MASS over the support point.

When walking a tightrope, the performer constantly corrects the balance, first seeming to lean to one side and correcting the lean, then seeming to lean toward the other side and correcting again. A pole makes the balancing easier. By moving the pole to the left or right, the walker can shift mass to one side or the other, keeping the center over the support point.

In addition, a long pole is better than a short pole and one that curves beneath is best of all. Why?

In order to fall, the center of mass must shift to one side above the support point. A short pole doesn't have to move very far to do that, but a long pole does, so the walker has plenty of time to make corrections. Look at the diagrams to see why a curved pole (or the dangling legs of the frog you built) works even better. A pole that curves makes balance even easier.

On the other hand, the diamond won't balance because you can't keep the center of mass over the support point.

Dough, Dough, Mold, and Go

Dough hardens in the air or in the oven because water leaves it. Water molecules are always in motion, so they can bounce away from the surface and escape into the air. This process is called EVAPORATION. The heat of the oven makes the molecules move faster, so evaporation goes faster, too. Any change in the state of matter (but not its character) is a PHYSICAL CHANGE. Boiling, melting, evaporation, and freezing of water are all examples of physical changes. The water changes form, but it is still water.

Physical changes are different from CHEMICAL CHANGES in which one substance is changed to another with different properties. That's what happens when you mix baking soda and vinegar. You get something different from what you started with. Your modeling dough is different from the water, flour, and oil

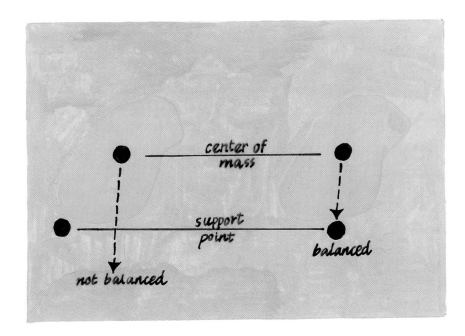

center of mass

support point

not balanced

balanced

you started with, too. Some definite chemical changes took place.

Bubbling Over

A bubble is a thin film of liquid filled with air. The shape of a bubble is the result of SURFACE TENSION. The surface of a liquid tends to "hold together" because the molecules are attracted to one another more strongly than they are to the air. You can see surface tension by floating a paper clip on water. (Yes, it can be done!) Look closely and you can see the surface of the water appearing to stretch beneath the paper clip. That same kind of tension holds bubbles together. When no other forces are pulling on the liquid film, bubbles form spheres.

Straight lines, angles, and geometric shapes form when the surface of one bubble pulls against the surface of another. That's why you got a cube inside a cube when you built your toothpick bubble frame.

When Green's Not Green

Mixing paints can produce new colors. The primary colors are blue, red, and yellow. Mix blue and red to get purple. Mix red and yellow to get orange. Mix blue and yellow to get green. But once colors mix, they can separate again.

Liquids "climb" paper strips because the molecules of the paper attract the molecules of the liquid. Different colors climb faster than others, sometimes because the molecule is lighter and sometimes because the attraction to the paper is stronger. That's why green food coloring separates into blue and yellow. On most paper, the blue climbs higher than the yellow. (The green area in the middle is where a little of the blue and yellow overlap.) Because the interaction between the molecules and the paper is different, the order reverses on brown paper towel. The yellow climbs higher, leaving the blue behind.

Chop-and-Glop

Put a little sugar in water, shake it up, and you make a SOLUTION. You can't see the sugar anymore, because it dissolved in the water.

Fine sand won't dissolve in water. Mix the two together, shake them up, and you'll still see the sand in the water. That's called a SUSPENSION. The particles of sand will settle to the bottom if you let the mixture sit long enough.

If the size of the particles is in between those of a solution and a suspension, then a COLLOID may form. A colloid is not a solution, but it's not a suspension either. It's in between the two. Some examples of colloids are gelatin desserts, milk, salad dressing, whipped cream, smoke, fog, smog, glue, and latex paint.

Milk is a colloid that acts like a liquid because it has a lot of water in it and because the solids it contains are very small. Plastics, gels, aerosols, and foams

are also colloids, although they don't always act like chop-and-glop. For example, some plastics are hard at room temperature, but they flow like a liquid when heated.

Leave chop-and-glop in the air for a day or two and the water evaporates into the air. EVAPORATION is the movement of water molecules into the air. It's the reason clothes dry on the line and puddles disappear after a rain storm. When the water in chop-and-glop evaporates, dry cornstarch remains behind. And, when you put cornstarch in hot water, lumps will form.

Your Nose Knows

We can smell odors because molecules floating in the air attach to certain cells in the nose. The more molecules, the stronger the smell. To prove it, open a bottle of perfume in one corner of a room. Move to the opposite corner. Can you smell the perfume? Wait a few minutes. How long does it take for the odor to reach you? If you ever get a chance, try this experiment in a room full of people. Ask your subjects to raise their hands the moment they

detect the perfume. You'll see the closest hands going up first, then the ones farther away joining in later.

We don't understand how the process works, but molecules bind to tiny hairs in the nose. This causes nerve cells to send a message to our brain. The brain somehow "decides" what the odor is and you react to it. That's why you do very different things when you smell cookies baking or pass a pile of rotting garbage.

Whirly-Giggle

Air is invisible, but you know it's there when you feel the wind, blow up a balloon, or watch a parachutist descend safely to earth. Have you ever put your flat palm out the window of a car and felt your hand rise as the car sped along? Even on a still day, the movement of the car creates what feels like a wind and you feel LIFT. Lift works against GRAVITY. Gravity is the attraction of one lump of matter for another. Since the earth is large and the whirly-giggle is small, gravity pulls the plane toward the earth's core. A whirly-giggle spins because two forces are at

work. Gravity pulls it down, while lift makes it "fly"—at least for a little while. Heavy objects like helicopters and jumbo jets can fly because their engines create lift to overcome gravity.

Undercover Work

When a bean embryo starts to grow, it gets food energy from the starchy material stored inside the bean. Roots grow down and stems grow up no matter how you turn the seed when you plant it. That response is called GEOTROPISM.

Another neat trick plants can perform is PHOTOTROPISM. That means they grow toward the light. Place a plant far from the window and notice how it grows. It will bend toward the light. It may grow tall, skinny, and pale from lack of light. A plant that has plenty of light will grow straight, compact, and green.

Plants store the energy of sunlight in sugars they make in their leaves. They need only water from the soil and carbon dioxide from the air to perform this feat. This process of making food is called

PHOTOSYNTHESIS.

Animals can't make food. They get energy by eating plants (or by eating animals that have eaten plants). Don't be confused by plant "foods" you can buy at the garden center. They contain minerals that may help plants stay healthy, but plants don't get energy-providing food from the soil. They make their own.

V-Room, V-Room

Energy is what it takes to move a weight from one point to another, which is what scientists call WORK. The more something weighs or the farther it moves, the more work is done. Not all the energy put into trying to move a weight ends up doing useful work. Some always gets changed to waste heat. AIR RESISTANCE and FRICTION are great energy robbers. As a car moves through the air, for example, some energy gets used in pushing the air aside to make room for the car (air resistance). The sleeker and more streamlined the car's silhouette, the more easily it pushes aside the air. Also, a car loses energy through the contact of the wheels with the road (friction). The smoother and rounder the wheels and the smoother the surface, the more easily the car moves. That means less energy is lost to friction and more actually ends up moving the car.

Leery Lizards

Many animals escape becoming another animal's dinner thanks to their camouflage, or PROTECTIVE COLORATION. Polar bears are hard to see in the snow, and brown-patterned snakes such as the copperhead look a lot like the leaf piles they hide in. The stick insect looks like a twig. The octopus, chameleon, squid, and cuttlefish not only gain protection by changing colors, but also the advantage in an attack.

Some animals are obviously not camouflaged at all. That may be because sending messages to others of their kind is more important to the survival of the species. Consider the male pheasant, for example. His bright colors let the female know he's nearby and ready for mating.

air resistance

friction

Seesaw, Swing, and Draw

Levers are SIMPLE MACHINES that make hard work a lot easier. They work because the weight multiplied by the distance on one side of the fulcrum equals the weight multiplied by the distance on the other side. Let's sup-

its swing to the other side. Scientists call this PO-TENTIAL ENERGY, or stored energy. As the pendulum drops, some of that potential energy changes to KINETIC ENERGY, or the energy of motion. As the pendulum swings up the other side, that kinetic energy changes to potential energy again. At the moment of its pause on the other side, the pendulum has as much potential energy as it started with.

How fast a pendulum swings has nothing to do with the weight of the pendulum, how hard it's pushed, or how high it swings. Only the length of the support makes a difference. Short pendulums swing quickly; long ones swing slowly.

Why does the pendulum stop swinging after a while? In a VACUUM (a space without air), it would keep swinging forever. It's only the resistance of the air that steals some of the energy from each swing and causes earthbound pendulums to slow down and stop.

pose you have a very heavy weight to lift. Where should you put the fulcrum?

Remember, the weight multiplied by the distance from the fulcrum equals the weight multiplied by the distance from the fulcrum on the other side, so the big weight needs only a little distance. If a lifter is pretty puny, he'll need to have a long lever length. So, when Archimedes said he would move the earth, he must have had something like this in mind:

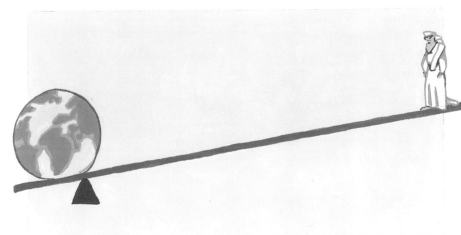

In the Swing

What happens when a pendulum swings? As it swings higher to one side, it moves more and more slowly. At the top of its swing, it stops for a fraction of a second, then starts back down again, moving faster and faster until it reaches the bottom of its swing. Then it starts up the other side and repeats the process, moving more and more slowly until it stops once more. The point is this: When it stops at the top, it has all the energy it needs to complete

I've Got Rhythm, You've Got Rhythm

Your pulse comes from your heartbeat. Every time your heart beats, it pushes a wave of blood through vessels called ARTERIES. You have arteries close to the skin at your wrist, temple, neck, and inside your elbow. That's why you can feel a pulse there.

The heart is a muscle, but it doesn't need messages from the brain to tell it to contract. It has its own command and control center called a PACE-MAKER, a bundle of cells that contract, sending a wave of contraction through the heart.

Chemicals in the body affect how fast the heart beats. For example, when you get scared, your adrenal gland releases adrenaline into your blood. Adrenaline causes your heart to beat faster. It readies your muscles for swift, strong action.

Messages from the brain can also speed or slow the heart rate. That's what happens when you exercise.

Like any muscle, the heart gets stronger with exercise. Couch potatoes have "flabby" heart mus-cles, so their hearts must beat faster to move blood through the body. Those in better shape have slower heart rates. They need fewer beats because their hearts are stronger and pump more blood with each beat.

In general, the smaller and lighter the person, the faster the heart rate. That's why children's hearts generally beat faster than adults', and women's hearts beat faster than men's.

Float Your Boat

Common sense suggests that heavy things sink and light things float. But that can't be right! The *Queen Mary* weighs as much as 14,000 elephants, and it floats, but a pin that weighs less than a cricket sinks. So what's the difference? Find out for yourself by getting two plastic containers. Margarine tubs will do, but make sure they are the same shape and size. Put one in some water, empty. Does it float? Place the other in the water and gradually add some weight. Coins work fine; sand or salt works even better. Watch what happens as you add weight, a little at a time. The tub gradually sinks in the water. Add more weight and eventually the water will rise to the very top of the tub's rim. Only a little more weight will sink the tub.

Things float or sink be-cause of the amount of space they take up (their VOLUME) *in relation to* their weight. This rela-tionship is called DEN-SITY. Your two tubs have the same volume; they take up the same space. But as you add weight, the density increases—that is, you pack more weight into the same space. If you add too much weight, the den-sity of the tub becomes greater than the density of the water, so your tub sinks.

In this experiment, you made clay float by chang-ing its shape. Actually, what you changed was its volume, the amount of space it took up. The weight stayed the same, but you made your boat less dense, so it floated. The *Queen Mary* weighs many tons, but its volume lets it float.

A Pound of Feathers and a Pound of Lead

The same VOLUME (space) of two different cereals may have a different weight because of DEN-SITY. (See the explanation above for "Float Your Boat.") Density is the MASS (amount of matter) in something in relation to its volume. Think about the pound of feathers and the pound of lead. They both weigh the same. That means they have the same mass. But they take up different amounts of space, so they have different volumes. Lead is dense because it packs a lot of mass into its volume. Feathers are less dense because they take up a lot of space with only a little mass. In the same way, some cereals are denser than others. They cram more weight into the same amount of space.

Light, Light, Burning Bright

Electricity is a flow of electrons. Electrons are tiny,

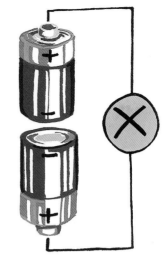

negatively charged particles that spin around in atoms. Electricity can only work if it travels in a complete circle, or CIRCUIT. The electrons have to come back to where they started. That's why the positive (+) and negative (−) ends on batteries are important. Batteries are a source of electrons.

Look at the drawing below. The bulb will light because the electrons flow in

a complete circle out of the battery and back again. As they flow through the bulb, they make it light up.

You can increase the amount of electricity that flows through the bulb (and make the light brighter) by using more batteries, but the circuit cannot be interrupted. This is the reason why some hookups work and others don't.

There are two kinds of simple circuits: series and parallel. Can you spot the difference?

Dyeing to Try It

Dyes work because molecules of the dye hang onto fibers of the fabric. The mordant changes the fibers so that they hold the dyes better and longer.

And the Music Goes Round and Round

Sound is vibration. Pluck a rubber band and listen to the sound. Touch the rubber band and feel the vibration. Fold a piece of tissue paper over a clean comb, place it between your lips, and blow. You'll hear the sound and feel the vibration.

There are three ways to make a stringed instrument, such as a cello, a violin, or your rubber band "guitar," play a higher pitch. One is to shorten the strings. Another is to use thinner strings. The third way is to increase the TENSION (tightness) on the strings. You used all three of these methods in your experiment.

Baby, It's Cold Outside

Things are hot or cold because of how fast their molecules move. In hot things, the molecules move very fast. The colder something is, the slower the molecules move.

When something hot comes in contact with something cold, the fast-moving molecules of the hot thing lose some of their energy to the cold thing. That makes the molecules in the cold thing move faster, so it warms up. When you put your hand in cold water, some of the heat from your hand transfers its energy to the cold water, so your hands feels cold.

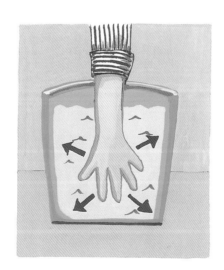

INSULATION forms a barrier between heat and cold. The barrier slows down the transfer of heat energy, so hot things stay hot and cold things stay cold. Rabbit fur insulates the animal against winter's chill. Gloves and mittens do the same for people.

The shape of the rabbit's body helps, too. A round, compact body loses less heat than a long thin one because it exposes less surface to the cold. That's why your palm stays warmer when you form a fist than when you open your hand.

Enzymes

Inside the cells of living things, many hundreds of chemical reactions go on all the time. These reactions wouldn't happen without ENZYMES. Enzymes are chemicals made by living things that speed up the reactions needed to keep life going.

Each enzyme has only one job. The enzyme called catalase chops an oxygen atom off the hydrogen peroxide molecule. In chemical symbols, H_2O_2 becomes H_2O (water) and O_2 (oxygen). It's the oxygen gas that makes the bubbles. This reaction happens in hydrogen peroxide on its own, but very slowly. The catalase in the cells of a living potato makes things go a whole lot faster.

Enzymes work best

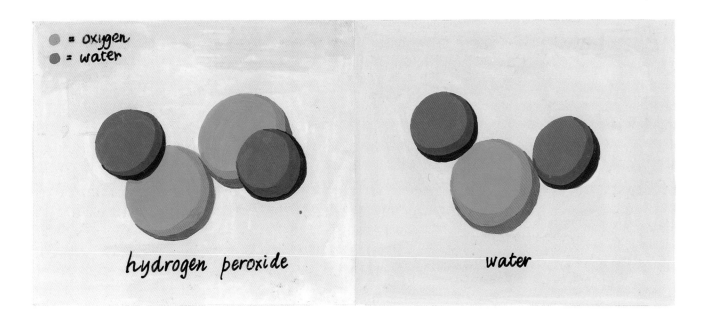

= oxigen
= water

hydrogen peroxide

water

when warm, but not too hot. Cooking destroys enzymes. Freezing cold can nearly stop enzyme action. That's why freezing stops food from spoiling.

Enzymes need enough of their "food," or SUBSTRATE, to work on. As you saw, a shortage of hydrogen peroxide slows bubble production.

Finally, enzymes need the right environment to work in. A strong acid or base (see "Berry, Berry, Not So Contrary") stops enzyme action.

Index